Mastering
the Art of
Chinese Cooking

Mastering the Art of Chinese Cooking

With step-by-step instructions

Charmaine Solomon

Photographer RAY JOYCE

WELDON
PUBLISHING
SYDNEY · LONDON

The Publishers would like to thank the following for
their kind assistance in lending us props for photography:
Doulton Tableware Pty Ltd, Gordon N.S.W.
Mikasa Tableware Pty Ltd, Glebe N.S.W.
Kosta Boda Australia Pty Ltd, Artarmon N.S.W.
Tee Jay Antiques, Willoughby N.S.W.
We'd particularly like to thank William Lai of
Asia Provisions Pty Ltd, Chatswood N.S.W.
for all his help in the preparation of this book.

Food styled by June Budgen

A Kevin Weldon Production

Published by Weldon Publishing
a division of Kevin Weldon & Associates Pty Limited
Sydney, Australia

First published by Lansdowne Press 1984
Reprinted by Weldon Publishing 1992

© Copyright: Charmaine Solomon 1984
© Copyright design: Kevin Weldon & Associates Pty Limited

Managing editor: Susan Tomnay
Editor: Beverley Barnes
Designer: Elaine Rushbrooke

Typeset in Australia by Griffin Press, Adelaide, in Plantin
Printed in Singapore by Kyodo Printing Co. (S'pore) Pte Ltd

National Library of Australia Cataloguing-in-Publication data

Solomon, Charmaine.
  Mastering the art of Chinese cooking, with step-by-step
instructions.

  Includes index.
  ISBN 1 86302 187 6.

  1. Cookery, Chinese. I. Joyce, Ray, 1947- . II. Title.

641.5951

Contents

Introduction

Chinese cooking has long been acknowledged as the most sophisticated of all the great cuisines. It is also the most ingenious.

The amazing variety of ingredients were first used in sheer necessity. The country has always been subject to drought and flood and only a small proportion of the land is suitable for agriculture, so the people have learned to make use of everything edible. Who else but the Chinese have made a delicacy from wood fungus, birds' nests and fish's maw?

Chinese food should appeal to all the senses. First there is visual impact. Colour and form are considered in the combination of ingredients and the shapes they are cut into. On special occasions, the Chinese delight in garnishes made from vegetables and representing flowers, butterflies, birds or animals. The fragrance of a dish is important, for before the food can give pleasure by its taste, it should whet the appetite with its aroma.

Some dishes are prized for the noise they make – such as sizzling rice – but it has other attractions – the crispness of the rice itself and the flavour of the sauce served with it.

A dissertation on texture ingredients in a classic essay on Chinese gastronomy differentiates between crunchy, smooth, elastic, chewy, soft, resilient, spongy, melting, grainy, unctuous, fibrous, gelatinous. Many of these qualities would be lost on even the most discerning western gourmet. Some of the most highly regarded foods are totally devoid of flavour but are prized because of their texture. Skilful cooking imbues them with appeal from the seasonings they are combined with.

Finally, and most important of all, is the taste of the food. There are many effects to strive for. Some dishes are supposed to be light, delicate and natural in flavour but without being insipid. Others are prized for their rich, concentrated flavour.

Choosing a menu

A Chinese meal does not feature one main dish, but rather a number of dishes of equal importance. A cleverly chosen menu presents contrasting dishes, so the qualities of each are set off by the others.

A formal banquet is served as a succession of courses with pauses in between for drinking, conversation and playing games – which explains how diners can partake of ten or more courses and how banquets can last for hours. Indeed, in times gone by they lasted for days!

When planning a Chinese menu, be guided by the rules that apply to western meals – don't repeat main ingredients or flavours, balance a rich dish with a light one, serve vegetables on their own if they are not featured with the meat or seafood. Remember that steamed rice is important because most Chinese dishes taste better with it.

Until you become really proficient in the split-second timing required for stir-frying, don't be tempted to present more than one dish cooked by this method. Include roasted, boiled and braised dishes that may be cooked ahead and reheated – not only because it's easier on the chef, but for more variety.

At family meals or for informal entertaining, all the dishes are placed on the table at once. This makes it unnecessary for the hostess to leave the table once the meal has started. Each person has a bit of each dish with rice. Soup is not served at the start of a meal, as in western-style eating, but in banquets is served between other courses. In family-style meals it is placed on the table and everyone helps themselves, just as they do with rice. It is not necessary to have one dish for each diner.

Above: *a Chinese place setting: bowl and porcelain spoon, bone plate, chopsticks on chopstick rest, sauce dishes.*

Right: *typical Chinese teapot and teacups. In background, cane basket for carrying teapot and keeping it warm.*

Right: *chopsticks with rests.*

Chinese place settings

Chinese food may be served in any dish of appropriate size, but for eating try to provide each person with a small bowl, and chopsticks and a porcelain spoon. It is easier to pick up food from a bowl than from a flat plate, and the 10 cm (4 inch) size does for both solid food and soups.

The bowl is placed on a small flat plate, which is the 'bone plate' – a place where the small bones may conveniently be discarded.

Small individual-size sauce dishes are useful and in some dishes quite essential, as the food is given flavour with the dipping sauce.

Porcelain spoons are favoured not merely because they can be bought in colours to match the bowls, but for the very practical reason that they do not get hot as metal spoons do and diners run less risk of burning their lips when supping the very hot soups. Chopstick rests are a nice touch, although not absolutely essential.

The Chinese teacup is small, without handles, and looks right for serving and drinking Chinese tea at the end of a meal. Hefty western-style cups with handles somehow don't seem appropriate.

If serving Chinese wine with the meal, it is usually served warm. Small flasks in which it can be warmed (by standing the flask in hot water) come with half a dozen wine cups in the set.

Cooking methods

Chinese cooking may, at first glance, appear difficult and far removed from everyday methods in a western-style kitchen.

But there are many cooking methods which are familiar to the western cook – boiling, braising, stewing, simmering, steaming, deep frying. Not as well known is cooking in stored heat, which takes longer but makes good sense because it saves fuel and yields good results.

Then there is the quick stir-frying method which always fascinates the newcomer to Chinese cooking. It looks very impressive but there is nothing to it except split-second timing and this is easily mastered with a little practice. All that is necessary is to have every ingredient prepared and ready within reach before starting to cook, because there is no time to go looking for a sauce or seasoning once cooking is under way.

It is for this method of cooking, in particular, that food is cut into paper-thin slices or slivers because the cooking time is so short. The principle is that the ingredients which require longer cooking go into the wok first, to be followed in turn by the others. It originated out of the need to save fuel, and that is as good a reason to use this method today as it was centuries ago.

Then there are recipes in which more than one method is used. This is called cross-cooking or combination cooking. A duck may be steamed until tender, then boned and cut into pieces and deep fried so that the outside is crisp and crackling, the inner portions meltingly soft. Or bite-size pieces of poultry, meat or seafood may be briefly deep fried and set aside, and just before serving they are stir-fried with other ingredients and seasonings.

Roasting is not a common cooking method in China, where homes do not have ovens and the method is too wasteful of fuel, but because oven cooking is so convenient in western kitchens, some restaurant recipes have been adapted for this book.

Utensils and preparation methods

With a sharp Chinese chopper, a heavy cleaver and a stout wooden chopping block, anyone can master the art of slicing, chopping and cutting in the Chinese way. Cleavers and choppers may look clumsy but they are surprisingly comfortable to handle and, as long as they are kept in good condition, are safe to use. A sharp knife is safer than a blunt one, providing it is used with an awareness of its sharp edge.

Chopping through bones is often called for in preparing poultry or meat. With a heavy cleaver held firmly where the handle joins the blade, and an unhesitating delivery, this task can be accomplished without difficulty. Since in this book we have the advantage of every recipe illustrated in photographs, there is no need to try to explain about diagonal cutting, shredding and other methods. Each one can be clearly seen.

A sturdy wooden chopping block or board is a must. Please do not use slick-surfaced lightweight chopping boards, no matter how decorative they are. Hang them on your kitchen wall if you must, but chop on solid wood. It will save your knife blades and save many a dangerous situation too, because its surface is not smooth and slippery. To be safe and effective the chopping block must be at least 5 cm (2 inches) thick and large enough to allow room to work freely.

There are different kinds of choppers. Stainless steel looks good but carbon steel holds a better edge and is easier to sharpen. A good compromise is the type in which the blade is of stainless steel enclosing a cutting edge of carbon steel. Like the wok, choppers must be washed and thoroughly dried before putting away, especially if made of carbon steel.

The most useful chopper is that with a large rectangular blade. The handle of the chopper is useful for pounding or crushing, taking the place of a pestle. The side of the blade is used for crushing garlic or flattening a circle of pastry to a thin, translucent sheet. The pointed corner takes over from the tip of the chef's knife. And the large rectangular blade is just the thing to carry cut ingredients from chopping block to wok.

Above: *wooden chopping boards and choppers.*

What to cook on

Quick, high, instantly controllable heat is what makes Chinese cooking a pleasure, so gas is therefore the most suitable fuel. But there are ways of using electricity to advantage. One is to buy a flat-bottomed wok – an invention which takes into account the fact that people in Asian countries who live in modern blocks of flats have to cook with electricity. The flat base gives better contact with the hotplate and prevents wobbling. The high, flaring sides of the wok enable the cook to toss, flip and stir without ingredients being scattered as may happen in a conventional frying pan or skillet.

Electricity is not flexible like gas, and different methods have to be used to achieve the same results. With an electric stove, heat one hotplate on the highest setting, put the wok on it and let it get very hot before adding the oil and ingredients to be cooked. When less heat is needed, lift the wok off the hotplate (turning the heat down would not reduce it quickly enough). If the dish needs simmering after the initial cooking on high heat, have another hotplate ready on simmer setting and transfer the wok to this.

If you can get only round-bottomed woks, use a metal collar or ring which will hold the wok in place and steady it. These rings are sometimes necessary even on gas stoves, depending on the design. It is essential you should feel confident that the wok is held steady.

The rings are usually made of anodized aluminium and are constructed with sloping sides so one opening is smaller than the other. There are holes in the ring to allow ventilation. When high heat is required, use the ring with the large opening upwards so that the wok sits close to the source of heat. When simmering, the smaller opening should be uppermost so that the wok is held higher up and further away from the heat.

If cooking for a number of people, remember to cook two batches of the dish rather than double the quantities. This applies to stir-fried dishes especially, for if too much is added to the wok at a time, the heat will not be sufficient to seal the juices in and the food will stew rather than fry.

What to cook in

There is no doubt that cooking Chinese food in a wok is as appropriate as eating Chinese food with chopsticks. While it is possible to cook Chinese food in other types of pans, the wok was designed specifically for Chinese cooking and really does make it easier. Especially when stir-frying, the high, flaring sides enable food to be stirred and tossed with speed and allows meat to be pressed against the hot metal to seal the surfaces. The food unmistakably tastes better.

Any Chinese cook will confirm that a well-used wok develops what is known as 'wok hay' – a sort of character of its own, which adds an extra dimension to food cooked in it, just as the well-aged clay pots used in some other countries give a special flavour to food.

Woks come in many sizes. I would recommend one 35 cm (14 inches) in diameter as being suitable for domestic use. It may look large and can cook enough for 6 to 8 people. Even if you don't usually cook for that many, consider that whereas you can cook small amounts in a large wok, you can't cook large amounts in a small wok.

Some woks have a long wooden handle, but the original design has two rounded handles and I find this easier to use when lifting the wok as the weight is more evenly distributed.

A word about those handles. They do get quite hot in the course of cooking. Chinese chefs use a cloth, folded many times to form a heatproof pad. It becomes second nature to them to reach for the wok with pads in hand, but for the amateur home cook it takes a bit of practice to remember. I take precautions by wrapping the metal handles in two or three layers of insulating tape. This way, even if I grab the handles, no blistered fingers result. After a couple of months of constant use, the tape does become tacky and must be replaced but it is a small chore well worth performing.

When buying a wok, don't imagine that the most expensive is the best. Forget the stainless steel or aluminium woks, the non-stick linings, all the gimmickry that crops up whenever something becomes popular. These are woks in name only. Look for the original iron woks, or the serviceable enamelled wok in our photographs. A 35 cm (14 inch) wok should weigh about 1 kg (2¼ lb). Those intended for use on electric hotplates are heavier in order to make good contact and have a small flat area in the base.

When new, a wok must be cleaned and seasoned. Most iron woks have a coating to prevent them rusting during transportation and storage. This is a stubborn film which must be removed by filling the wok with hot water and adding 2 tablespoons of bicarbonate of soda (baking soda); bring to the boil and simmer for 20 minutes. This softens the coating which can then be scrubbed off with a fine scourer. Repeat the process if necessary. This is the first and last time you should scour the wok.

Seasoning the wok

Having cleaned the wok thoroughly, season it. This is very important because it creates a smooth surface which prevents food from sticking, becoming discoloured, or absorbing a metallic taste from the 'raw' metal.

Heat the wok and wipe over the entire inner surface with a wad of kitchen paper dipped in peanut oil. At first, the paper will turn rusty and brown. Repeat with more paper and more oil. After a number of times the paper will

Below: *wok and bamboo brush for cleaning wok.*

not become brown. Allow the wok to cool, rinse it with warm water, then repeat the heating and rubbing with oil as before.

The wok is now ready to cook in. Remember the rule, 'hot wok, warm oil'. Make sure the wok is thoroughly heated before adding the oil, and wait for the oil to become hot before adding ingredients. Then food will not stick to the wok but will slide easily over the surface.

After use, wash the wok in hot water and scrub it gently with a dish mop or sponge. Do not scour with steel wool or scouring powder. If necessary, fill it with hot water and leave it to soak and soften any food that may have cooked on, then scrub with a brush.

The wok should always be completely dry before it is put away. To ensure this, place it over the source of heat until any moisture has completely vaporized. **Wiping with a dish cloth is simply not enough.**

If not used often, the wok should be wiped over lightly with a piece of kitchen paper dipped in peanut oil to prevent rust, but only after it has been dried over heat. Don't store the wok in a closed cupboard – it would develop a musty odour. Hang it near the stove, both to keep it in usable condition and to remind you how versatile a utensil it is, for frequent use.

Wok accessories and other utensils

When you buy a wok, buy a lid for it too. It is necessary when braising, simmering or steaming, and should fit snugly inside the wok. Choose a high dome-shaped lid as this will accommodate larger items such as a whole duck or chicken. These lids are generally made from lightweight aluminium and dent easily, so treat with care.

Above: *nest of bamboo steaming baskets.*

Other accessories are a steaming rack or steaming baskets. The former is a simple arrangement of bamboo, wood or metal which holds food above water level. A wire cake rack (round, of course) is a good substitute.

Steaming can be done in a large saucepan if you have one with a well-fitting lid. The plate of food is placed on a trivet or an upturned heatproof bowl to hold it above water level. The plate should be of a size that allows steam to circulate.

For steaming more than one kind of food at a time, it is best to use an aluminium steamer with multiple layers, or a nest of bamboo steamers. The bamboo steamers are particularly useful if you want to cook dim sum – dumplings, buns and patties. The woven bamboo lid with its natural perforations prevents condensation forming on the inner surface, falling on to the buns and spoiling their appearance. This can happen with metal steamers, but placing a clean dry tea towel across the top before covering with the lid solves the problem of condensation.

A sandy pot, or earthenware casserole, is ideal for slow-simmered dishes and is quite picturesque for presenting food in. The outside is a creamy colour and the inside is glazed dark brown. It comes in varying sizes and with one or two handles. It should not be placed over heat without first putting some liquid in it. When ingredients have to be browned first, this is done in a wok and they are then transferred to the pot for simmering.

The Yunnan pot is another beautifully shaped cooking vessel which has an unusual feature – a small funnel in the centre which allows steam into the pot. I love its rounded shape and the way it cooks the most delicately flavoured soup.

Then there is the steamboat (hotpot) which cooks at the table from live coals piled into its central funnel. Small wire cooking spoons are used to suspend pieces of food in the simmering stock, or wooden chopsticks may be substituted to hold the food as it cooks. An electric deep fryer or electric wok or a tabletop cooker with a vessel on it may be used instead, but for atmosphere and authenticity there's nothing to beat the steamboat itself, even if it is more trouble filling the chimney with live coals than simply plugging in and flicking a switch. Remember to have the coals prepared an hour or more beforehand so that they are well aglow before transferring them to the steamboat; and have the moat filled with stock before doing so.

Cooking implements

There is a frying spoon called a wok chan which is shaped to fit into the curve of the wok. It is exactly right for the tossing, flipping and pressing motions that take place during stir-frying. Stainless steel is the most suitable metal. When transferring food from the wok, the slight curve on its leading edge and the upturned edges on the other two sides make it very practical. A curved frying spoon may be substituted, but because of the slots it is not as useful in transferring cooked food and sauces.

A ladle is handy because it doubles as a measure. Choose one which holds 125 ml (4 fl oz). Once the eye is trained to levels in its bowl, it can be used to speedily dip out stock or water in the amounts required.

For deep frying, a large twisted-wire draining spoon with flat wooden handle is extremely useful. Buy one large enough to hold a whole fish. It is handy for smaller items as well. When frying small pieces of food, it is easy to skim them out on this strainer.

There is another shape of twisted-wire spoon – a deep cup shape, which is used for holding food such as noodles or dumplings in bubbling broth until heated and lifting all the food out at once, as in wonton soup.

Below: *from left: sandy pot, woks with draining rack and lid, wire frying spoons and cup-shaped wire ladle for dipping noodles, metal ladle, wok chan, wooden rice spoon.*

Appetizers and Savoury Snacks

Most formal banquets start with appetizers. A trend that has also become popular, even when having just a simple meal in a Chinese restaurant, is to assuage the pangs of hunger until the main dishes arrive by ordering a plate or two of hot dim sum. These are usually enclosed in fine pastry and either steamed or fried.

Originating with the chefs of the Sung Dynasty, these little mouthfuls were intended as delicacies and culinary showpieces to impress guests. Dim sum literally means 'touch the heart'. Gradually they were aspired to by the merchant class and eventually by the working class. Now they are so popular with all manner of people that in Chinese cities (or Chinese quarters of western cities) whole families, from grandparents to babes in arms, gather at restaurants on a Sunday morning especially, for yum cha (tea) or dim sum brunch.

The concept of a dim sum meal grew up around the Chinese tea house where people met to talk, read newspapers, or simply refuel. I have been at dim sum restaurants as early as seven in the morning and have been told that the trade starts at about 4 a.m. as Chinese workers from night shifts come in for cup after cup of hot tea and an endless variety of small savoury dishes. By eight in the morning, these places close. It is then that the more elegant restaurants start serving their dim sum to the leisured classes who rise later. At working-class tea houses the dim sum are actually quite hearty, not dainty as at fashionable restaurants.

Waitresses circulate among the crowded tables with trolleys or trays bearing steaming baskets, plates and bowls. In them or on them is an incredible variety of dim sum. Customers look them over and choose whatever appeals, and at the end of the meal the waitress counts the empty dishes and calculates the bill.

The recipes in this chapter are for some of the most popular appetizers and snacks. Shaping the pastries may require a little practice, but that applies to most pastries, Chinese or otherwise.

Left: *clockwise from left: Steamed dumplings; Chinese mushrooms; bean sheets; water chestnuts; red vinegar for dipping; Prawn dumplings in Transparent Pastry (see page 16); chilli sauce for dipping; sesame seeds; Steamed Pearl Balls (see page 29); bottles of oyster sauce and sesame oil; lump sugar; Spring Rolls (see page 24).*

Deep Fried Chicken and Ham Rolls

Remove skin from the chicken breasts, and with a sharp knife, bone the breasts. Divide each whole breast in two down the middle. On the underside of the flesh, next to the bone, there is a small cylindrical fillet which lifts off easily; reserve this for another dish. Put the large pieces of breast between two sheets of freezer polythene and pound until thin, using the smooth side of a meat mallet and taking care not to tear the flesh.

Combine salt, five spice powder and garlic; spread this evenly on the inside of each piece of breast.

Cut the ham into sticks 12 mm (½ inch) wide and the length of the chicken breast. Shave the corners to round the sticks. Place a stick of ham on each piece of breast and roll up to enclose the ham completely, moulding the chicken flesh to seal.

Dip in the beaten egg, then into the flour. Put diagonally on a spring roll wrapper, roll over twice, then fold in the corners, envelope fashion. Seal the pastry with a little beaten egg mixed to a thick paste with flour.

Heat 1 litre (1¾ pints) of oil in a wok and fry two rolls at a time for about 3 or 4 minutes, turning the rolls with tongs so that they brown evenly. Drain on absorbent paper.

Cut into diagonal slices and arrange on a bed of shredded lettuce. Serve with Sweet and Sour Sauce for dipping, if liked.

Sweet and Sour Sauce: The red food colouring powder is available from Chinese food stores, and only the smallest amount is required. Place the sugar and vinegar in a small saucepan. Add 175 ml (6 fl oz) water and bring to the boil. Use a skewer to put a small quantity of the food colouring into the sauce. Blend cornflour with 15 ml (1 tbsp) cold water and stir this into the sauce until it boils and thickens. Add salt and mix in well.

Serves 6–8
2 large chicken breasts
1.25 ml (¼ tsp) salt
1.25 ml (¼ tsp) five spice powder
1.25 ml (¼ tsp) crushed garlic
1 slice ham 12 mm (½ inch) thick
2 eggs, beaten
flour for coating
4 large sheets spring roll pastry
oil for deep frying
shredded lettuce for serving
Sweet and Sour Sauce:
100 g (4 oz) sugar
125 ml (4 fl oz) white vinegar
red food colouring powder
1 tablespoon cornflour
1.25 ml (¼ tsp) salt

Bone the chicken breasts.

Place ham stick on flattened chicken breast.

Fold corners of wrapper over chicken roll.

Prawn Toast

Serves 6

6 square slices white bread
225 g (8 oz) raw prawns
1 egg, beaten
2.5 ml (½ tsp) finely
  grated fresh ginger
2.5 ml (½ tsp) salt
15 ml (1 tbsp) oyster sauce
10 ml (2 tsp) cornflour
sprigs of fresh coriander
  (Chinese parsley)
30–45 ml (2–3 tbsp)
  sesame seeds
peanut oil for deep frying

Serve as a tasty appetizer with drinks, as part of a meal, between courses, or as a snack.

Trim the crusts off the bread, cut each slice in half diagonally or into three strips, and leave on a tray for an hour or two to dry out a little.

Shell and de-vein the prawns. If using frozen prawns, thaw completely and drain off any liquid. Chop the prawns very finely and place in a bowl. Add 15 ml (1 tbsp) of the beaten egg, the ginger, salt, oyster sauce and cornflour; mix well to blend to a smooth paste.

Spread the bread with prawn mixture. Press a sprig of coriander on some of the pieces. Brush other pieces lightly with the remaining beaten egg, and dip in sesame seeds to coat.

Heat the oil for deep frying and when hot, put in a few pieces of bread at a time, prawn side downwards. Fry until the bread is golden, lift out on wire spoon and allow to drain on absorbent paper. Serve hot.

Cut bread into strips.

Spread bread with prawn mixture.

Dip some of the bread into sesame seeds.

Prawn Dumplings in Transparent Pastry

Flatten slice of dough with Chinese chopper.

Flute and join edges of dough.

Steam dumplings on oiled greaseproof paper in Chinese basket.

Filling: Shell and de-vein the prawns and cut into small pieces. Combine with all the other ingredients for the filling, mixing thoroughly. Set aside while making the dough.

Dough: Mix the Chinese wheat flour and cornflour together in a bowl. Put the measured water and the lard into a small saucepan and bring to the boil. Remove from heat and cool while counting 20 seconds, then pour all at once on to the flour. Mix well with chopsticks or the handle of a wooden spoon, and as soon as it is cool enough to handle, knead to a smooth, pliable dough.

Divide into two equal portions and mould each into a cylinder 2.5 cm (1 inch) in diameter. Wrap the dough in plastic film to prevent the surface drying out.

Cut one of the cylinders of dough into 10 equal slices and re-cover these with plastic wrap. On a smooth surface (a laminated pastry board is ideal), flatten one dough slice with the lightly greased blade of a wide Chinese chopper to a round about 10 cm (4 inches) in diameter.

Put 5 ml (1 tsp) of filling on the dough. Bring the edges of the dough together over the filling, pinch to seal, and at the same time flute the joined edges on one side so that the dumpling has the shape of a bonnet. (Don't worry if the shape is not perfect, it will still taste marvellous!) Repeat with remaining dough and filling.

Brush the dumplings lightly with sesame oil and place each one on an oiled square of greaseproof paper. Steam for 12 minutes. Serve warm, with sauces for dipping.

Makes 20
Filling:
225 g (8 oz) raw prawns
30 ml (2 tbsp) finely chopped ham fat
30 ml (2 tbsp) finely chopped canned bamboo shoot
2 spring onions, finely chopped
2.5 ml (½ tsp) finely grated fresh ginger
15 ml (1 tbsp) cornflour
5 ml (1 tsp) sesame oil
5 ml (1 tsp) salt
5 ml (1 tsp) sugar
Dough:
100 g (4 oz) Chinese wheat flour
60 ml (4 tbsp) cornflour
210 ml (7 fl oz) water
20 ml (4 tsp) lard
sesame oil for brushing

Butterfly Prawns

Slit prawns along back, flatten gently.

Coat with cornflour, egg and breadcrumbs.

Shell and devein the prawns, leaving the tails intact.

With a sharp knife, slit the prawns along curve of the back but do not cut right through. Flatten gently. Combine soy sauce, wine, garlic crushed with salt, ginger. Marinate the prawns in this mixture for 15 minutes.

Dip the prawns into cornflour, shake off excess, then dip into the beaten egg and finally into the breadcrumbs. Press gently to flatten the prawns again and to firm on the crumb coating. Chill for 30 minutes.

Heat a wok, add oil and when hot, fry the prawns, two or three at a time, until golden brown (about 2 minutes). Drain on kitchen paper and serve hot, with chilli sauce if desired.

Serves 4–6
12 large raw Dublin Bay prawns
45 ml (3 tbsp) light soy sauce
20 ml (4 tsp) Chinese wine or dry sherry
1 small clove garlic, crushed
1.25 ml (¼ tsp) salt
2.5 ml (½ tsp) finely grated fresh ginger
50 g (2 oz) cornflour
1 large egg, beaten
breadcrumbs for coating
peanut oil for deep frying

Steamed Dumplings

Makes about 24
**6 dried Chinese
   mushrooms**
**450 g (1 lb) small raw
   prawns**
6 canned water chestnuts
3 spring onions
**60 ml (4 tbsp) chopped
   canned bamboo shoot**
225 g (8 oz) minced pork
7.5 ml (1½ tsp) salt
**20 ml (4 tsp) light soy
   sauce**
**20 ml(4 tsp) Chinese wine
   or dry sherry**
5 ml (1 tsp) sesame oil
1 egg white
**100 g (4 oz) wonton
   wrappers**

Place the mushrooms in hot water; soak for 30 minutes.

Peel the prawns, reserve about 24 for garnish, and chop the remainder. Drain the mushrooms; slice off and discard their stems. Chop the mushroom caps, water chestnuts and spring onions. Combine the chopped ingredients with bamboo shoot, pork, salt, soy sauce, wine, sesame oil and egg white; mix well together.

Put 10 ml (2 tsp) of the mixture in the centre of each wonton wrapper. Gather the wrapper around the filling and press it together to give the shape of a little money bag, open at the top. Press a reserved prawn on top of each for decoration.

Lightly oil a steamer and place the dumplings in a single layer on the perforated tray. Cover tightly and steam for 20 minutes over boiling water. Serve hot or cold, with a dipping sauce of soy or chilli.

Chop the mushrooms, water chestnuts and spring onions.

Place mixture on wonton wrapper.

Form dumpling into money bag shape.

Chicken and Ham wrapped in Lettuce

Serves 6–8
3 dried Chinese
  mushrooms
450 g (1 lb) chicken thighs
1 chicken liver
100 g (4 oz) ham
1 egg
5 ml (1 tsp) cornflour
20 ml (4 tsp) light soy
  sauce
75 ml (5 tbsp) finely
  chopped canned
  bamboo shoot
2 spring onions, finely
  chopped
5 ml (1 tsp) finely grated
  fresh ginger
45 ml (3 tbsp) sweet bean
  paste (tim mein jeung)
2.5 ml (½ tsp) salt
1 round lettuce
15 ml (1 tbsp) peanut oil

Soak the mushrooms in hot water for 30 minutes. Then discard the stems and finely chop the caps.

Remove skin and bones from the chicken. Halve the liver and remove any tubes and discoloured spots. Finely chop the chicken, liver and ham in a food processor or with a chopper. Beat the egg and in a bowl combine the minced mixture, beaten egg, cornflour and soy sauce. Cover the bowl and set aside.

In a separate bowl, combine the chopped mushrooms, bamboo shoot, spring onions and the ginger.

In a third (small) bowl, stir 45 ml (3 tbsp) of water into the sweet bean paste and add the salt.

Wash the lettuce leaves, trim to a neat shape, wrap in a clean towel, and chill.

Heat a wok, add oil and when hot, stir-fry the chicken mixture for about 3 minutes or until its colour changes. Add vegetables and stir-fry a further 2 minutes. Add the bean paste mixture and stir well together.

Serve the hot filling in a large bowl and the chilled lettuce leaves on a platter or large bowl. Place a spoonful of the mixture on a lettuce leaf, roll up and eat. It is quite in order to use the fingers for this dish.

Note: If liked, fry 60–75 ml (4–5 tbsp) of pine nuts in oil until golden, then toss them in with the filling after it has been cooked.

Finely chop the mushrooms, bamboo shoots, spring onions and ginger.

Mix the bean paste with water.

Vegetarian Dumplings

Finely chop the prepared gluten.

Add the cabbage to the wok with the other vegetables.

Makes about 24

240 g (8 oz) cooked and minced gluten (see page 53)
4 dried Chinese mushrooms
45 ml (3 tbsp) peanut oil
4 spring onions, finely chopped
5 ml (1 tsp) crushed garlic
5 ml (1 tsp) finely grated ginger
100 g (4 oz) finely chopped Chinese cabbage (wongah bak)
10 water chestnuts, chopped
15 ml (1 tbsp) light soy sauce
10 ml (2 tsp) sesame oil
5 ml (1 tsp) salt (or to taste)
1 large egg, beaten
20 ml (4 tsp) cornflour
100 g (4 oz) wonton wrappers

Prepare the gluten and when cool, squeeze out excess water and mince in food processor or chop finely.

Soak the mushrooms in hot water for 30 minutes. Then discard the mushroom stems and finely chop the caps.

Heat a wok, add the peanut oil and when the oil is hot, fry the spring onions, garlic and ginger, stirring, for a few seconds until fragrant. Add the cabbage and toss until cabbage is soft. Add water chestnuts, mushrooms and gluten and toss for a minute or two, then transfer the mixture to a large bowl.

Mix together the soy sauce, sesame oil, salt, beaten egg and cornflour. Pour over the gluten mixture and mix well with your hand to distribute the seasonings and bind together.

Place 20 ml (4 tsp) of the mixture in the centre of each wonton wrapper, gather the wrapper to enclose the filling and squeeze the dumpling firmly to make the dough adhere to the filling. Press the points down with the back of a teaspoon.

Place the dumplings in an oiled steamer and steam for 10 minutes. Serve warm, or refrigerate until needed and reheat by steaming for a couple of minutes.

Press points of dumpling with the back of a teaspoon.

Golden Cuttlefish Balls

Serves 6

75 g (3 oz) **very tiny bread
  cubes**

450 g (1 lb) **cleaned
  cuttlefish (or squid)**

5 ml (1 tsp) **salt**

5 ml (1 tsp) **sugar**

5 ml (1 tsp) **sesame oil**

1 litre (1¾ pints) **oil for
  deep frying**

Dipping Sauce:

125 ml (4 fl oz) **white
  vinegar**

125 ml (4 fl oz) **water or
  pineapple juice**

30 ml (2 tbsp) **sugar**

15 ml (1 tbsp) **tomato
  purée**

2.5 ml (½ tsp) **salt**

5 ml (1 tsp) **cornflour**

To prepare the bread cubes, trim the crusts off several thin slices of day-old bread and cut into thin strips, then into tiny dice no more than 4 mm (1/8 inch) each way.

Wash the cuttlefish well and remove any of the fine membrane that may be clinging to the flesh. Chop the cuttlefish finely or mince in food processor using steel chopping blade. Transfer to a bowl and mix in the salt, sugar and sesame oil. Take teaspoons of the mixture and roll into small balls about 2 cm (¾ inch) in diameter.

Spread the bread cubes on a sheet of paper and roll the cuttlefish balls in them until they are covered.

Heat the oil and deep fry the balls, a few at a time, until golden; do not overcook. Drain on absorbent paper and serve warm, with sauce for dipping if liked.

Dipping Sauce: Heat vinegar, water (or pineapple juice), sugar, tomato purée and salt in a small saucepan. When boiling, stir in the cornflour mixed smoothly with 15 ml (1 tbsp) of cold water. Cook, stirring, until it boils and becomes thick and clear.

Note: Squid may be substituted for cuttlefish. And if a hot sauce is preferred, serve a dip of bottled chilli sauce.

Remove the cuttle-bone.

Roll the cuttlefish balls in the bread cubes.

Pot Stickers

Place the mushrooms in hot water; soak for 30 minutes.

Discard the mushroom stems, and chop the caps finely. Finely chop the spring onions, add to the pork, and mix in the mushrooms, bamboo shoot, ginger, salt, soy sauce and sesame oil. Blend the cornflour with 30 ml (2 tbsp) of cold water and add it to pork mixture, mixing all well together.

Dough: Measure the flour into a large bowl. Pour in the boiling water, stirring with chopsticks (or the handle of a wooden spoon) for a few minutes. As soon as it is cool enough, knead the dough well until it is soft and smooth, dusting with flour if necessary.

Shape the dough into a log, then roll it on a smooth surface into a sausage shape 2.5 cm (1 inch) in diameter. Slice it evenly into 30 pieces. Cover with a damp cloth to prevent it drying.

On a lightly floured board, roll each piece of dough to a circle 8 cm (3¼ inches) in diameter. Make overlapping pleats around one side of the circle. Place 5 ml (1 tsp) of the filling in the centre. Dampen the edges of the dough with water, and pinch them together to seal. Keep the dumplings under a damp cloth but not touching each other as they would stick.

Heat a large heavy flat-bottomed frying pan over a medium heat. Add 40 ml (8 tsp) of the peanut oil and when hot, tilt the pan to coat its entire base and a little way up the side. Add half the dumplings, pleated side up. (It is easier to cook them in two batches.) Lift the dumplings with a flat spatula to prevent them sticking, and cook until they are golden underneath.

In a saucepan bring to the boil 250 ml (8 fl oz) of water and 40 ml (8 tsp) of the oil, and pour this over the dumplings. Loosen any that are sticking. Bring the liquid to the boil again, cover the frying pan and cook for 5 minutes; then reduce the heat and cook for a further 5 minutes. Remove the frying pan lid, and cook until liquid evaporates and the dumplings are browned and crusty underneath. Lift the dumplings to prevent sticking.

Cook the remaining dumplings in the same way (using the remaining oil and an extra 250 ml (8 fl oz) of water).

Serve with chilli sauce, soy sauce or red vinegar for dipping.

Pleat one side of dough circle.

To prevent sticking, lift dumplings with spatula.

Makes 30

4 dried Chinese
  mushrooms
4 spring onions
225 g (8 oz) minced pork
30 ml (2 tbsp) finely
  chopped canned
  bamboo shoot
2.5 ml (½ tsp) finely
  grated fresh ginger
2.5 ml (½ tsp) salt

10 ml (2 tsp) light soy
  sauce
10 ml (2 tsp) sesame oil
10 ml (2 tsp) cornflour
160 ml (5½ fl oz) peanut
  oil, for cooking
Dough:
225g (8 oz) plain flour
250 ml (8 fl oz) boiling
  water

Cloud Swallows (Deep Fried Dumplings)

Place the mushrooms in hot water; soak for 30 minutes.

Drain the mushrooms, squeeze out excess moisture, trim off and discard the stems and chop the caps finely. Chop the prawns and spring onions. Combine mushrooms, prawns, spring onions, bamboo shoot, minced pork and seasonings; mix well together.

Put a small amount of filling about 2.5 ml (½ tsp) in the centre of each wonton wrapper. Moisten the edges of the dough with water, fold over to a triangle with points slightly overlapping and press together. Then bring the two ends together, dab with a little of the filling mixture where they join and press to seal.

When all are made, deep fry a few at a time on medium heat until golden (about 2 minutes). Serve as an appetizer or as part of a meal with sweet and sour sauce.

Makes about 40
6 dried Chinese mushrooms
100 g (4 oz) raw prawns
4 spring onions
60 ml (4 tbsp) finely chopped canned bamboo shoot
225 g (8 oz) minced pork
7.5 ml (1½ tsp) salt
15 ml (1 tbsp) light soy sauce
5 ml (1 tsp) sesame oil
225 g (8 oz) wonton wrappers
peanut oil for frying

Dried and soaked mushrooms.

Fold dough over filling into a triangle with overlapping points.

Join two ends of triangle together.

Spring Rolls

Cut pork into fine shreds.

Place filling at one end of each wrapper.

Roll wrapper, folding in ends to enclose filling

Traditionally eaten on New Year's Day and again in the spring, Spring Rolls (also known as Egg Rolls in America) can be easily made at home using the frozen wrappers which are available from Chinese stores and delicatessens.

Slice the pork thinly and then cut into fine shreds. Shell, de-vein and finely chop the prawns. Chop the water chestnuts and spring onions. Pinch the tails from the bean sprouts. Shred crisp leaf ribs of the cabbage to give 225 g (8 oz).

Heat a wok, add half the peanut oil and fry the garlic and ginger over low heat until fragrant (do not brown). Add the pork, increase the heat and stir-fry until it changes colour. Add prawns and continue stirring until they are cooked. Remove from the wok to a large mixing bowl.

Heat the remaining peanut oil in the wok and fry the vegetables for 2 minutes. Add the sauces and salt. Make a space in the centre and stir in cornflour mixed with 15–30 ml (1–2 tbsp) of cold water. Stir until the sauce boils and thickens. Remove from the wok to the pork-prawns mixture. Add the sesame oil and mix well. Allow to cool.

Put 30–45 ml (2–3 tbsp) of the filling at one end of each spring roll wrapper and roll it up, turning in the ends so that the filling is completely enclosed. Dampen the edges with water and press to seal.

Heat plenty of oil in a wok and fry the spring rolls a few at a time until golden. Drain on absorbent paper, and serve immediately with chilli sauce.

Makes 20
225 g (8 oz) pork fillet
450 g (1 lb) raw prawns
12 water chestnuts
6 spring onions
100 g (4 oz) bean sprouts
1 small Chinese cabbage
45 ml (3 tbsp) peanut oil
2.5 ml (½ tsp) crushed garlic
2.5 ml (½ tsp) grated fresh ginger
15 ml (1 tbsp) light soy sauce
15 ml (1 tbsp) oyster sauce
5 ml (1 tsp) salt
15 ml (1 tbsp) cornflour
5 ml (1 tsp) sesame oil
1 packet frozen spring roll pastry, thawed in wrapping
peanut oil for deep frying

Shanghai Dumplings

Mix together the pork, salt, soy sauce, wine, finely chopped spring onions and grated ginger. Slowly beat in 60 ml (4 tbsp) of water. This makes the filling juicy.

Measure flour into a bowl, make a well in the centre and pour in 125 ml (4 fl oz) cold water. Using the handle of a wooden spoon or chopsticks, mix to a dough, working from the centre and gradually incorporating the flour. Turn on to a lightly floured surface and knead for 5 to 6 minutes. The dough will become very smooth.

On the floured surface, roll the dough thinly and cut about 24 rounds 6 cm (2½ inches) in diameter. Place a small teaspoonful of the meat mixture in the centre of each round. Make two 'box pleats' on one side of the circle. Dampen the edges with water and seal them together to make dumplings.

Bring a large saucepan of water to the boil, add the dumplings and when they rise to the top and the water bubbles furiously, add 250 ml (8 fl oz) of cold water. Once more let the water bubble up, then add another 250 ml (8 fl oz) of cold water. This keeps the dough firm and prevents bursting. Serve hot, with Chinese red vinegar and light soy sauce for dipping.

Makes about 24
300 g (11 oz) minced pork
2.5 ml (½ tsp) salt
5 ml (1 tsp) light soy sauce
5 ml (1 tsp) Chinese wine
 or dry sherry
2 spring onions
2.5 ml (½ tsp) grated
 ginger
175 g (6 oz) flour
Chinese red vinegar for
 dipping
light soy sauce for dipping

Knead dough until very smooth.

Make two box pleats on one side of the dough circle.

Seal moistened edges to form dumpling.

Glazed Chicken Wings

Serves 4–6

700 g (1½ lb) chicken
   wings
3 spring onions, cut into
   5 cm (2 inch) lengths
5 ml (1 tsp) grated fresh
   ginger
60 ml (4 tbsp) Chinese
   wine or dry sherry
75 ml (5 tbsp) dark soy
   sauce
10 ml (2 tsp) lump sugar,
   crushed
1.25 ml (¼ tsp) ground
   Szechwan pepper
15 ml (1 tbsp) sesame oil

Remove the tips from the chicken wings and divide the wings at the joint. Put the wings into a saucepan of water to cover, and bring to the boil.

Drain, return the wings to the saucepan and add all other ingredients except sesame oil. Bring to the boil, then reduce the heat and simmer covered for 20 minutes, or until the chicken meat is tender. Turn the wings occasionally so that they are evenly coated with the sauce.

Remove the chicken wings to a plate. Reduce the sauce by cooking uncovered until thick. Turn off the heat, return the wings to the saucepan, sprinkle with the sesame oil and leave to cool. Serve at room temperature.

Remove tips from wings.

Divide chicken wings at joint.

Crush the rock sugar.

Steamed Egg Roll

Serves 8

Filling:

175 g (6 oz) chicken, raw
    prawns or lean pork
2.5 ml (½ tsp) salt
10 ml (2 tsp) light soy
    sauce
2.5 ml (½ tsp) sesame oil
5 ml (1 tsp) cornflour
15 ml (1 tbsp) finely
    chopped fresh coriander
15 ml (1 tbsp) finely
    chopped spring onion

Wrappers:

5 eggs
2.5 ml (½ tsp) salt
15 ml (1 tbsp) peanut oil
5 ml (1 tsp) sesame oil

Filling: Put the chicken, prawns or pork into an electric blender with salt, soy sauce and sesame oil and blend until smooth. Because the mixture is thick, it will be necessary to switch the blender on and off frequently and move the mixture on to the blades with a spatula. Then scrape it into a bowl and mix in the other ingredients, combining well. Alternatively, chop everything very, very finely with a sharp chopper until it has the consistency of a paste or use a food processor.

Wrappers: Beat the eggs well with salt. Reserve about 15 ml (1 tbsp) of beaten egg for sealing the egg rolls.

Heat a small omelette pan. Measure the peanut and sesame oils into a saucer. Dip a piece of absorbent kitchen paper in the oil and grease the pan. Pour 45–60 ml (3–4 tbsp) of egg mixture into the pan and make a thin omelette, cooking it on one side only; turn it on to a plate. Repeat with remaining egg mixture, greasing the pan each time. There will be 4 or 5 omelettes, depending on the size of your pan.

Divide the filling into the same number of portions as there are omelettes. Place each omelette on a board, cooked side up, and spread the filling almost to the edges using an oiled spatula or back of a spoon. Roll up like a Swiss roll and seal the edges with reserved beaten egg.

Lightly oil a plate with the mixed oils and place the rolls on it. Set the plate in a steamer (or on a rack in a saucepan of boiling water), cover and steam for 15 minutes. (The plate needs to be smaller than the steamer to allow steam to circulate.)

Remove from the steamer, allow to cool a little, then cut into slices diagonally. Serve hot or cold.

Make a thin omelette, cooking on one side only.

Spread filling on cooked side of omelette, almost to edges.

Place egg rolls on a plate in a steamer.

Bean Starch Sheets and Crystal Chicken

Wash the chicken breasts. In a pan that will be large enough to hold them in one layer, pour just enough water to almost cover the chicken pieces. Add ginger, spring onions and salt. Bring the water to the boil and then add the chicken pieces. Return to the boil, cover the pan, and cook for 3 minutes. Then turn the pieces over and cook for a further 3 minutes. Turn off the heat and allow to stand in the covered pan for 15 minutes. Remove the chicken pieces, allow them to cool, and then chill. (Save the chicken stock for another dish.)

Soak the sheets of green bean starch in hot water for 20 minutes. Then boil them for 5 minutes. Drain and refresh under cold running water. Cut into strips 5 cm (2 inches) × 1 cm (½ inch). Drain thoroughly and chill.

String the beans and cut them into diagonal strips. Drop them into boiling water to which has been added the peanut oil, and boil rapidly for 2 minutes. Drain and allow to cool.

Combine the sauce ingredients; in cold weather it may be necessary to warm the sesame paste to mix.

Remove the chicken meat from the bones and cut it into shreds. Arrange the strips of green bean starch on a platter, top with chicken meat and beans, and serve with the sauce spooned over. Serve on a bed of crisp lettuce leaves. If liked, garnish with fresh coriander.

Serves 4–6
4 chicken breasts
few slices of fresh ginger
2 spring onions
2.5 ml (½ tsp) salt
3 bean sheets
225 g (8 oz) French beans
15 ml (1 tbsp) peanut oil
Sauce:
30 ml (2 tbsp) Chinese sesame paste
15 ml (1 tbsp) sesame oil
30 ml (2 tbsp) dark soy sauce
30 ml (2 tbsp) Chinese wine or dry sherry
15 ml (1 tbsp) chilli sauce
15 ml (1 tbsp) Chinese sweetened vinegar
10 ml (2 tsp) sugar

Sheets of green bean starch.

Cut the cooked bean sheets into strips.

Steamed Pearl Balls

Serves 6
225 g (8 oz) rice
6 dried Chinese
  mushrooms
225 g (8 oz) minced lean
  steak
225 g (8 oz) minced pork
3 spring onions, finely
  chopped
2.5 ml (½ tsp) finely
  grated fresh ginger
2.5 ml (½ tsp) crushed
  garlic
7.5 ml (1½ tsp) salt
1 small egg, beaten
60 ml (4 tbsp) finely
  chopped canned water
  chestnuts

Soak the rice in cold water to cover for at least 2 hours. Then drain well and spread it on paper towels to absorb excess water while preparing meatballs.

Soak the mushrooms in hot water for 30 minutes. Then squeeze out excess water, discard the stems and chop the caps finely. Put into a large bowl with all the remaining ingredients and mix very well with your hand so that the seasonings are evenly distributed. With wet hands shape into balls 2.5 cm (1 inch) in diameter.

Roll each ball separately in the rice, with enough pressure to make the rice stick and coat the ball.

Put the balls on a lightly oiled steamer rack or bamboo steamer, leaving a little space between because the rice will swell. Steam over fast boiling water for 30 to 35 minutes, adding more boiling water as water boils away. The rice swells and the balls will be covered with pearly grains when done. Serve with a dipping sauce of soy sauce flavoured with a few drops of chilli oil or sesame oil.

Note: If you do not have a steamer, improvise with a large pan that has a well-fitting lid. Put the pearl balls on a heatproof plate small enough to allow the steam to rise around it, and place the plate on a trivet or upturned bowl which will hold it above water level.

Roll meatballs in soaked rice.

Place in a lightly oiled steamer.

Cold Appetizer Platter

This consists of a selection of cold Chinese appetizers: Sweet Sour Mustard Cabbage, Marinated Abalone, Steamed Chicken Pâté, Braised Mushrooms with Garlic and Barbecued Pork (see page 110). Serves 6.

Sweet Sour Mustard Cabbage: Cut the mustard cabbage (gai choy) into chunks. Place the vinegar, salt and sugar in a saucepan, add 350 ml (12 fl oz) water, and bring to the boil. Add oil, and boil the cabbage for 1 minute. Drain and chill.

Sweet Sour Mustard Cabbage:
- 1 bunch Chinese mustard cabbage (gai choy)
- 125 ml (4 fl oz) vinegar
- 5 ml (1 tsp) salt
- 10 ml (2 tsp) sugar
- 15 ml (1 tbsp) peanut oil

Cut the Gai Choy into chunks.

Marinated Abalone: Drain the abalone, cut into thin slices and place in a bowl. Combine the soy sauce, sugar, wine, sesame oil and ginger, pour it over the abalone and chill for 2 hours.

Drain the abalone and reserve the marinade to serve as a dip.

Marinated Abalone:
- 425 g (15 oz) can abalone
- 75 ml (5 tbsp) light soy sauce
- 15 ml (1 tbsp) sugar
- 15 ml (1 tbsp) Chinese wine or dry sherry
- 15 ml (1 tbsp) sesame oil
- 2.5 ml (½ tsp) finely grated fresh ginger

Cut abalone into thin slices.

Steamed Chicken Pâté: Skin and bone the chicken breast. Scrape the flesh to a purée using a sharp chopper (as described in the recipe for Chicken Velvet Fu Yung, on page 87), adding 10 ml (2 tsp) of water while puréeing. Alternatively grind finely in a food processor.

Mix in the salt, pepper, ginger, spring onions, coriander leaves, cornflour and egg white.

Lightly oil a bowl with peanut or sesame oil, and pack the chicken pâté into the bowl, smoothing the top. Place in a bamboo steamer or on a rack in a pan of boiling water and steam for 10 minutes or until set.

Allow to cool completely. Turn out of the bowl, cut in half, then slice each half neatly into even slices. Arrange on a serving platter.

Serve with a dipping sauce of 45 ml (3 tbsp) of dark soy sauce mixed with 2.5 ml (½ tsp) of sesame oil.

Steamed Chicken Pâté
- 350 g (12 oz) chicken breast
- 2.5 ml (½ tsp) salt
- pinch of ground white pepper
- 1.25 ml (¼ tsp) finely grated fresh ginger
- 30 ml (2 tbsp) finely chopped spring onions
- 30–45 ml (2–3 tbsp) finely chopped fresh coriander
- 5 ml (1 tsp) cornflour
- 1 egg white, slightly beaten

Scrape the chicken flesh to a purée.

Braised Mushrooms with Garlic: Soak the mushrooms in 350 ml (12 fl oz) of hot water for 30 minutes. Drain, and squeeze water from mushrooms (reserve the soaking liquid). Discard the stems.

Heat a wok, add peanut oil and when hot, fry the garlic and ginger until fragrant. Add mushroom caps and fry, pressing their undersides against the wok until they are golden brown.

Add the reserved mushroom liquid, the soy sauce, sugar and sesame oil. Cover with a lid, and simmer for 30 minutes or until liquid is absorbed and the mushrooms take on a shiny appearance.

Discard garlic and ginger, and serve mushrooms hot as an accompanying vegetable or cold as part of a cold appetizer selection.

Braised Mushrooms with Garlic:
- 25 g (1 oz) dried Chinese mushrooms
- 45 ml (3 tbsp) peanut oil
- 1 large clove garlic, bruised
- 3 slices fresh ginger
- 45 ml (3 tbsp) dark soy sauce
- 15 ml (1 tbsp) sugar
- 10 ml (2 tsp) sesame oil

Press undersides of mushrooms against wok until golden.

Soups

In a Chinese meal, soup is not served at the beginning as in a western meal. For family meals, the soup is placed in the centre of the table together with the rice, and diners help themselves between other dishes. (This may explain why the Chinese table is always round.)

In a banquet, the soups (there is often more than one) are brought on as a change of pace between other courses. Some of the soups are light and clear, others are thick and robust in flavour. Some soups are prestige courses – intended to impress because of the rarity of ingredients and their cost. Shark fin soup and birds' nest soup fall into this category.

Soup is regarded as important nourishment for new mothers or invalids. Soup can also be a complete light meal when it is a noodle soup or one with dumplings, popularly known as long soup and short soup, respectively. Even the simplest soup should be based on strong stock that is home-made.

Stock

For chicken stock, use a chicken weighing about 1.4 kg (3 lb) and add 2 litres (3½ pints) water, 3–4 thick slices of fresh ginger, 2–3 spring onions and 10 ml (2 tsp) salt. The chicken should be stripped of extra fat near the tail, the tail removed and discarded. It is then jointed, and carefully washed to remove traces of internal organs and blood. To these basic ingredients I like to add a dozen or so whole black peppercorns and a small sprig of celery leaves, but these are optional. Bring to the boil, then reduce the heat to a gentle simmer, and skim the surface until the broth is clear. Cover and cook on very gentle heat for 2 hours or more.

If liked, and for reasons of economy, some of the chicken joints may be lifted out after they are just cooked, and used in another dish such as cold chicken with sesame sauce. For the same reasons of economy instead of using a whole chicken, the bones saved from preparing meat for other recipes may be collected and frozen; then when there is sufficient, stock may be made from them. Freeze stock in quantities suited to family requirements and there is always the basis of a good soup on hand.

After the stock has cooked, strain it and add salt to taste. A dash of dry sherry or Chinese wine may be added if liked. Chill and remove any fat from the surface, though a little fat may be left to give the soup more richness.

For a meat stock, use 900 g (2 lb) meaty pork bones and proceed as for chicken stock, but use twice as much ginger and spring onions to combat the stronger flavour of the meat. Chill, and remove fat from the surface.

Left: *clockwise from left: spring onions; straw mushrooms; eggs; soy sauce; bundles of egg noodles; chilli oil; carrot and Chinese cabbage, cut into lengths; wonton, ready to cook, Wonton Soup (see page 34); Long Soup with King Prawns (see page 37); bean starch noodles.*

Wonton Soup

Serves 6
100 g (4 oz) raw prawns
100 g (4 oz) minced pork
2 spring onions, finely
   chopped
2.5 ml (½ tsp) salt
15 ml (1 tbsp) light soy
   sauce
1.25 ml (¼ tsp) crushed
   garlic
1.25 ml (¼ tsp) finely
   grated fresh ginger
100 g (4 oz) wonton
   wrappers
1.5 litres (2½ pints) stock
60 ml (4 tbsp) finely
   chopped fresh coriander
   or spring onions

In some restaurants this is known as 'Short Soup', the name referring to the dumplings as opposed to the long strands of noodles in 'Long Soup'.

Shell and de-vein the prawns and chop them finely. Mix with the pork, spring onions, salt, soy sauce, garlic and ginger.

Place a scant 5 ml (1 tsp) of the mixture on each square of wonton pastry. Moisten the edges, fold diagonally over the filling to make a triangle and press the edges together to seal. Moisten the two corners at the base of the triangle and join them together.

In a saucepan, bring a large amount of lightly salted water to a rolling boil and add a dash of oil. Drop in the dumplings, a few at a time, and after the water has returned to the boil, cook them for 5 minutes; add a small glass of cold water and bring to the boil again. Drain in a colander. Repeat until all dumplings are cooked.

Bring the stock to the boil, add the dumplings and return to the boil once more. Sprinkle with chopped coriander or spring onions, and serve hot.

Fold pastry diagonally over filling and seal.

Fold corners across and seal.

Wonton ready to be cooked.

Szechwan Soup

This is a rich, robustly flavoured soup which is served in smaller than usual bowls.

Soak the mushrooms in hot water for 30 minutes; then drain (reserve the liquid), discard the mushroom stems, and slice the mushroom caps finely. Soak the wood fungus in water for 10 minutes; then trim off any gritty portions and cut the fungus into small pieces. Soak noodles in hot water for 15 minutes, drain and cut into short lengths.

Heat 15 ml (1 tbsp) of oil in a wok and fry the mushrooms and pork, stirring constantly, until they start to brown. Add the dark soy sauce, sugar and 125 ml (4 fl oz) of the mushroom water. Simmer, covered, until the mushrooms have absorbed almost all the liquid. Add prawns and bean curd, and stir-fry for 1 minute.

Bring the stock to a boil, add the noodles and return to the boil; simmer for 5 minutes. Add the light soy sauce, vinegar, wine, chilli oil and the fried mixture. Mix the cornflour smoothly with 45 ml (3 tbsp) of cold water, and stir into the soup until it boils and thickens.

Dribble the beaten eggs into the simmering soup, stirring constantly so the egg separates into fine shreds. Season to taste with pepper and salt. Put a spoonful of wood fungus in each soup bowl and pour a ladle of the boiling soup over. Serve immediately.

Serves 6–8
8 dried Chinese
  mushrooms
15 ml (1 tbsp) dried wood
  fungus (cloud ears)
50 g (2 oz) bean starch
  (transparent) noodles
15 ml (1 tbsp) oil
125 ml (½ cup) finely
  chopped cooked pork
15 ml (1 tbsp) dark soy
  sauce
10 ml (2 tsp) sugar
100 g (4 oz) chopped
  prawns
1 square fresh bean curd,
  diced
1.5 litres (2½ pints)
  chicken or pork stock
15 ml (1 tbsp) light soy
  sauce
15 ml (1 tbsp) Chinese
  sweet vinegar
15 ml (1 tbsp) Chinese
  wine or dry sherry
5 ml (1 tsp) chilli oil
30 ml (2 tbsp) cornflour
2 eggs, beaten
salt and pepper to taste

Dried and soaked wood fungus.

Bean starch noodles.

Add the bean curd to the pork mixture.

Sung Dynasty Fish Soup

Chinese broccoli

Cut the fish into paper thin slices.

Immerse the fish and broccoli in oil for 10 seconds.

Serves 4

3 dried Chinese mushrooms
100 g (4 oz) sea bass fillets
2 stems Chinese broccoli (gai larn)
50 g (2 oz) barbecued pork (see page 110)
oil for deep frying
1 litre (1¾ pints) stock
15 ml (1 tbsp) shao hsing wine or dry sherry
salt to taste
30 ml (2 tbsp) cornflour mixed with a little cold water
1 egg white, slightly beaten

Soak the mushrooms in hot water for 20 minutes. Discard the mushroom stems, and steam the mushroom caps for 15 minutes. Slice finely.

Cut the fish into paper-thin slices. Cut the stems of broccoli diagonally into very thin slices. Cut the barbecued pork into thin slices, then into small squares.

Heat the oil in a wok for deep frying and when very hot, immerse the fish and broccoli on a wire frying spoon for about 10 seconds only. This is long enough to cook both fish and broccoli if they are sliced thinly, and the quick heat turns the broccoli a vivid emerald green. Drain.

Heat the stock in a saucepan and when boiling, add wine, fish, broccoli, mushrooms and pork. Taste, and add salt if necessary. Add the cornflour mixture a little at a time, stirring constantly, until the soup is thick and clear.

Finally, dribble in the egg white which will set into shreds. The entire cooking process should take only a few minutes. Serve immediately.

Long Soup with King Prawns

Place the mushrooms in hot water; leave to soak for 30 minutes. Remove and discard the mushroom stems and slice the caps finely.

Shell and de-vein prawns, but leave the prawn tails on.

Soak the noodles in hot water to loosen the strands, then cook them just until tender in lightly salted boiling water. Rinse in cold water, and drain.

Bring the stock to the boil, add the shredded cabbage and the noodles and stir in sesame oil and salt to taste. Turn off the heat and leave while cooking the prawns.

Heat the peanut oil in a wok and gently fry the garlic and ginger for a few seconds. Add the prawns and toss on high heat, stirring constantly for 2 to 3 minutes or until they change colour. Add the sliced mushrooms and soy sauce, and stir. Remove from heat.

Ladle the hot noodle soup into individual bowls. Place a portion of prawns on top of each serving, and garnish with sprigs of fresh coriander if desired.

Serves 6
450 g (1 lb) large raw
 Dublin Bay prawns
8 dried Chinese
 mushrooms
200 g (7 oz) fine egg
 noodles
1.5 litres (2½ pints) prawn
 or chicken stock
salt to taste
¼ Chinese cabbage
 (wongah bak), shredded
5 ml (1 tsp) sesame oil
45 ml (3 tbsp) peanut oil
2.5 ml (½ tsp) crushed
 garlic
2.5 ml (½ tsp) finely
 grated fresh ginger
15 ml (1 tbsp) light soy
 sauce

Shred the Chinese cabbage

Loosen noodles while soaking so they cook evenly.

Pork and Prawn Ball Soup

Serves 6
Pork balls:
225 g (8 oz) minced pork
**1.25 ml (¼ tsp) finely
grated fresh ginger**
**1.25 ml (¼ tsp) crushed
garlic**
2.5 ml (½ tsp) salt
**15 ml (1 tbsp) finely
chopped spring onion**
Prawn balls:
225 g (8 oz) raw prawns
**1.25 ml (¼ tsp) finely
grated fresh ginger**

1.25 ml (¼ tsp) salt
**1 slice soft white bread,
crumbed**
5 ml (1 tsp) cornflour
Soup:
**1.5 litres (2½ pints) pork
or chicken stock**
**15 ml (1 tbsp) Chinese
wine or dry sherry**
15 ml (1 tbsp) cornflour
2.5 ml (½ tsp) sesame oil
**30 ml (2 tbsp) finely
chopped spring onion**

Pork balls: Combine all ingredients, and form into balls the size of a large marble. Bring the stock to the boil, drop in the pork balls and return to the boil. Simmer for 15 minutes. Meanwhile make the prawn balls.

Prawn balls: Shell and de-vein the prawns and chop them very finely. Combine with all other ingredients, and form into balls the same size as the pork balls. Drop the prawn balls into the simmering stock after the pork balls have cooked for 15 minutes. Return to simmering point, cook for a further 3 minutes.

Stir in the wine, then the cornflour mixed with 15 ml (1 tbsp) of cold water. Boil, stirring, until the soup is clear and slightly thickened (about 1 minute). Stir in the sesame oil and serve, garnished with the spring onion.

Combine ingredients for pork balls.

Roll into marble-sized balls.

Prawn Velvet and Mushroom Soup

Wash and drain the prawns. Remove shells and heads, but simmer these in the stock for extra flavour, strain.

Remove any sandy veins and chop the prawns very finely until almost a purée, gradually adding 15 ml (1 tbsp) of cold water while chopping. Blend the 15 ml (1 tbsp) of cornflour with 15 ml (1 tbsp) of cold water and the salt, then combine this with prawn purée. Beat the egg whites until stiff and fold in. This may be done beforehand and the prawn velvet refrigerated.

Drain the mushrooms and slice them. Combine the 30 ml (2 tbsp) of cornflour with the wine, soy sauce and sesame oil.

Bring the stock to the boil, add the sliced mushrooms and the cornflour mixture, and stir until the soup boils and thickens. Add the prawn velvet and the frozen peas, and allow the soup to reach a gentle simmer once more. Taste and adjust seasoning if necessary; serve at once.

Serves 6

450 g (1 lb) raw prawns
15 ml (1 tbsp) cornflour
5 ml (1 tsp) salt
3 egg whites
1.25 litres (2 pints) stock
1 small can straw mushrooms or champignons
additional 30 ml (2 tbsp) cornflour
30 ml (2 tbsp) Chinese wine or dry sherry
15 ml (1 tbsp) light soy sauce
10 ml (2 tsp) sesame oil (optional)
25 g (1 oz) frozen peas

Chop prawns until almost a purée.

Fold stiffly beaten egg whites into prawn purée.

Shark Fin Soup

Slice chicken breast finely.

Add contents of the can of shark fin to stock.

Serves 6–8
6 dried Chinese
  mushrooms
1 large chicken breast
2 litres (3½ pints) strong
  chicken stock
225 g (8 oz) canned shark
  fin
15 ml (1 tbsp) light soy
  sauce
60 ml (4 tbsp) Chinese
  wine or dry sherry
60 ml (4 tbsp) cornflour
1 egg, slightly beaten
2 thin slices cooked ham,
  cut into matchstick
  strips

Soak the mushrooms in hot water for 20 minutes. Discard the mushroom stems and slice the caps very thinly, then cut the slices into fine strips.

Skin and bone the chicken breast; slice it as finely as possible.

Bring the stock to the boil with the shark fin, soy sauce and Chinese wine. Add the mushrooms and chicken, and when it returns to the boil, stir in the cornflour mixed with 45 ml (3 tbsp) of cold water. Cook, stirring, until it boils and thickens slightly. Dribble in beaten egg and stir so that the egg sets in fine shreds. Garnish the soup with ham, and serve at once.

Note: If preferred, substitute 225 g (8 oz) flaked crab-meat for the chicken.

Shanghai Egg Pouch Soup

Serves 6–8

100 g (4 oz) bean starch
   (transparent) noodles
6 dried Chinese
   mushrooms
half a Chinese cabbage
   (wongah bak)
2 litres (3½ pints) chicken
   stock

Egg Pouches:

100 g (4 oz) minced pork
1 spring onion, finely
   chopped
1.25 ml (¼ tsp) finely
   grated fresh ginger
2.5 ml (½ tsp) salt
5 ml (1 tsp) cornflour
3 eggs
pinch of salt

Swirl beaten egg in ladle over flame to coat evenly.

Fold one side of pouch over filling and seal.

This main-dish soup can be made more elaborate by adding slices of egg roll (page 27) or barbecued pork (page 110).

Soak the noodles in hot water for 20 minutes; then drain. Soak the mushrooms in hot water for 30 minutes; then drain, discard the stems and cut the caps into quarters. Wash the cabbage and cut it into thick slices.

To make the pouches: Combine the pork with the spring onion, ginger, salt and cornflour; mix well. In a separate bowl, beat the eggs with 15 ml (1 tbsp) of cold water and a pinch of salt.

Lightly oil a ladle and hold it over low gas flame. Pour in about 45 ml (3 tbsp) of the beaten egg, and swirl to give an even, thick coating of egg; pour excess egg back into the bowl. Put 5 ml (1 tsp) of the pork mixture on one side of the egg and fold the other side over, sealing the edge if necessary with a little of the uncooked egg. Continue making pouches until all the egg is used up. The pouches can be made in a heavy frying pan but the shape will not be as good. Place on a plate when made.

Cooking the soup: Heat the stock in a clay pot or flame-proof casserole, and season with salt if necessary. Add noodles, return to the boil and simmer for 5 minutes. Arrange the egg pouches in the pot and simmer for a further 5 minutes. In the centre place the sliced cabbage and the mushrooms, and give the soup a final 5 minutes' simmering.

Note: This dish can be prepared beforehand, to the stage where the noodles have been cooked in the soup. Have the egg pouches, cabbage and mushrooms ready in the refrigerator. About 20 minutes before serving, reheat the soup and continue with the recipe.

Crab and Corn Soup

Serves 6

225 g (8 oz) crabmeat,
 fresh or frozen
1 litre (1¾ pints) chicken
 stock
30 ml (2 tbsp) cornflour
283 g (10½ oz) can
 creamed sweetcorn
15 ml (1 tbsp) light soy
 sauce
30 ml (2 tbsp) Chinese
 wine or dry sherry
salt and white pepper to
 taste
10 ml (2 tsp) sesame oil
30 ml (2 tbsp) finely
 chopped spring onion
30 ml (2 tbsp) chopped
 fresh coriander leaves

Pick the crabmeat out of its shell if using fresh cooked crab, or thaw if using frozen crab. Flake the crabmeat and discard any bony pieces.

Bring the stock to the boil. Mix the cornflour smoothly with 45 ml (3 tbsp) of cold water and stir this into the stock until it boils and thickens. Add the corn, soy sauce, wine, and salt and pepper to taste. Add the flaked crabmeat and heat through.

Turn off the heat and stir in the sesame oil. Sprinkle with chopped herbs, cover the pan with a lid for 1 minute, then serve.

Note: A variation is to use canned abalone instead of crab. Slice the abalone thinly, then shred it finely. Add it at the last minute, only heating through, because cooking can toughen it.

Flake the crabmeat and discard any bony pieces.

Duck and Lettuce Soup

Serves 4
1 litre (1¾ pints) duck
   stock
100 g (4 oz) diced cooked
   duck
salt to taste
30 ml (2 tbsp) cornflour
half a small lettuce
1 spring onion
10 ml (2 tsp) white vinegar
dash of chilli oil
   (optional)
5 ml (1 tsp) sesame oil
5 ml (1 tsp) Chinese wine
   or dry sherry

A well flavoured stock is essential for Chinese soups. Duck stock has a distinct flavour and is made by simmering the neck and carcass of duck in water with 2 or 3 slices of fresh ginger and a spring onion. This is simmered for about 2 hours to extract as much flavour as possible. Even the bones of cooked ducks can be used to make stock, which is then strained and can be frozen for future use.

Bring the stock to the boil, add the cooked duck meat and salt to taste. Mix the cornflour smoothly with 15 ml (1 tbsp) of cold water and stir this into the stock until it thickens slightly and becomes clear.

Shred the lettuce, first cutting it in two lengthways so that the shreds will not be inconveniently long. Slice the spring onion in fine diagonal slices.

Remove the soup from heat and add the lettuce, spring onion, vinegar and (optional) chilli oil. Taste for seasoning, and add salt if necessary. Cover the pan and leave for 2 minutes. Then stir in sesame oil and wine, and serve the soup at once.

Finely shred the lettuce.

Cut spring onions into fine diagonal slices.

Yunnan Pot Chicken Soup with Winter Melon

Yunnan Pots are useful, decorative and not too expensive. Made from smooth red clay, the special feature is the narrow funnel which conducts steam up and into the pot. No liquid is added, but the dish makes its own strong, clear stock. Another version of this soup is made in a Chicken Pot—a covered pot with special base. Among those who can afford it, only the broth is used after prolonged steaming; the chicken pieces are discarded.

Soak the mushrooms in hot water for 30 minutes. Then squeeze out excess water, discard the stems, and cut the caps into halves or quarters. Rinse the chicken, cut off and discard the tail and excess fat. Cut the bird in half down the centre.

Remove thighs and drumsticks and pull off the skin. Chop the legs into 5 or 6 pieces, but do not cut through the joint. Remove the skin from the breast and cut each half of the breast into 4 pieces. Chop off wing tips (keep wing tips, neck and back for stock) and cut each wing into 3 pieces, again leaving the joint intact.

Put the chicken pieces into the pot and add ginger and spring onions. No water is needed in a Yunnan pot, but add a small amount (about 250 ml or 8 fl oz) to a pot that does not have a funnel.

Choose a saucepan just large enough to hold the Yunnan pot *above* water level when it has 5–7.5 cm (2–3 inches) of water in it. Bring to the boil and place the Yunnan pot on it. (If using the Chicken Pot or ordinary covered casserole, place in a large pan with hot water to come half-way up the casserole. Cover the pan with lid.)

Cook on medium high heat, keeping the water boiling briskly and adding more water as required, for 1½ to 2 hours.

Add peeled melon cut into chunky pieces, and cook for a further 10 minutes or until the melon is transparent. At the end of cooking, discard the spring onions and any large pieces of ginger. Stir in the wine, soy sauce, sesame oil and salt.

Serve the soup in the pot and accompany with steamed rice. Provide small individual sauce bowls for dipping the pieces of chicken in a flavouring sauce before eating.

Dipping Sauce: Mix equal parts of light soy sauce and Chinese wine or dry sherry with a few drops of sesame oil or a little finely grated fresh ginger, or toasted and crushed sesame seeds. For those who prefer a hot flavour, offer chilli sauce.

Serves 6
6 large dried mushrooms
1.4 kg (3 lb) roasting chicken
10 ml (2 tsp) shredded fresh ginger
2 spring onions
225 g (8 oz) winter melon

30 ml (2 tbsp) Chinese wine or sherry
15 ml (1 tbsp) light soy sauce
2.5 ml (½ tsp) sesame oil
2.5 ml (½ tsp) salt

Chop chicken leg into 5 or 6 pieces.

The peeled winter melon is cut into chunky pieces.

Mock Birds' Nest Soup

The dried fish maw.

Scrape chicken breast to a fine paste using cleaver.

Serves 6
25 g (1 oz) dried fish maw
1 chicken breast
2 egg whites
1.5 litres (2½ pints)
    chicken stock
salt to taste
60 ml (4 tbsp) cornflour
60 ml (4 tbsp) finely
    chopped canned water
    chestnuts
45 ml (3 tbsp) finely
    chopped ham

Birds' nests are one of the luxury ingredients served at Chinese banquets and illustrate how prestigious foods are chosen, not for their flavour but for their rarity and high cost. Since these swifts' nests have to be gathered from high almost-inaccessible cliffs, they are both rare and expensive. They are almost without flavour, being spun by the bird from its own saliva, but since they contain predigested seaweed are probably nutritious. The little nests need careful cleaning to rid them of feathers and dirt, and all in all it is easier to get the banquet effect by substituting fish maw.

This may sound almost as weird, but is a fascinating ingredient to work with, being the lining of a fish's stomach which is thoroughly cleaned and dried, then deep fried so that it puffs up like a balloon. It has to be soaked and cut into fine shreds and has no fishy smell or taste—a good example of a texture ingredient. Since the flavours in this soup are so delicate, I suggest using a strong-flavoured ham such as prosciutto to add interest.

Soak the fish maw in very hot water and put a weight on top to hold it down. When cool, squeeze out all the water and cut into fine shreds.

Remove skin and bones from the chicken breast, scrape to a fine paste, as in the recipe for Chicken Velvet Fu Yung (page 87), adding 20 ml (4 tsp) of cold water to lighten, then folding in the stiffly beaten egg whites.

Bring the chicken stock to a boil, add salt to taste. Add the shredded fish maw and simmer for 5 minutes. Mix the cornflour with 15 ml (1 tbsp) of cold water to a smooth consistency and stir it into the stock until it thickens slightly and becomes clear. Add the water chestnuts. Stir in the chicken velvet, then remove from the heat. Ladle into a tureen, sprinkle the ham over, and serve.

Vegetables

Vegetables are important in Chinese meals. Meat or poultry dishes are often combined with vegetables so they will feed more people than they would if meat were used alone. This also makes for healthier eating than would 'heavy meat' dishes which are more suitable for banquets.

When cooked Chinese style, vegetables retain all their goodness and have the additional appeal of crisp texture and heightened colour. Not until the 'nouvelle cuisine' of recent years has any other cuisine approached the Chinese style of cooking vegetables.

In addition to purely vegetable dishes, there are those that are combined with proteins such as gluten 'steaks' and bean curd – the latter is known in China as the meat without bones. These are ideal for vegetarian diets and, served with rice or noodles, make a complete and well-balanced meal.

In some of the following recipes, small amounts of meat or seafood are added, more as a flavouring ingredient than as the major component.

Left: *clockwise from left: Chinese cabbage (wongah bak); ginger; choy sum; red pepper; Chinese (garlic) chives; dried mushrooms; green pepper; Chinese mustard cabbage (gai choy); spring onions; chillies; bean sprouts; mange-tout; garlic; asparagus; fried bean curd.*

Asparagus in Oyster Sauce

Use the freshest asparagus for Chinese dishes. Tender asparagus spears will snap crisply if they are fresh.

Wash the asparagus spears, slice off and discard any tough ends. Bring plenty of water to boil in a wok. Add the oil and drop in the asparagus. Return the water to the boil and cook for 10–15 minutes, or until the asparagus spears are tender but still crisp.

Lift the asparagus out of the water on to a board and cut the spears into 5 cm (2 inch) lengths. Arrange on a serving dish.

Discard the asparagus cooking water. Put 60 ml (4 tbsp) of cold water in the wok, stir in the oyster sauce and bring to the boil. Pour it over the asparagus and serve immediately.

Serves 4

2 bundles fresh asparagus
15 ml (1 tbsp) peanut oil
15 ml (1 tbsp) oyster sauce

Lower asparagus spears into rapidly boiling water.

Cut cooked asparagus into lengths.

Braised Chinese Cabbage

Trim the cabbage, discarding tough leaf portions, and cut into bite-size pieces. Heat the peanut oil, and fry the garlic and ginger for a few seconds, then add cabbage and stir-fry for 1 minute. Add the stock and sauce, cover and cook for 3 to 4 minutes, just until tender but still crisp. Stir in the cornflour, first mixed with 15 ml (1 tbsp) cold water. Sprinkle with sesame oil, toss well and serve.

Cut cabbage into bite-sized pieces.

Add stock and sauce to lightly fried cabbage.

Serves 4

450 g (1 lb) Chinese
   cabbage (wongah bak),
   trimmed
60 ml (4 tbsp) peanut oil
2.5 ml (½ tsp) crushed
   garlic
2.5 ml (½ tsp) finely
   grated fresh ginger
125 ml (4 fl oz) stock
15 ml (1 tbsp) oyster sauce
   or light soy sauce
10 ml (2 tsp) cornflour
5 ml (1 tsp) sesame oil

Braised Broccoli Stems

Peel the broccoli stems, cut them into bite-size lengths, and cut any thick stems in half. Bring lightly salted water to the boil in a saucepan, drop in the stems and return to the boil, then cook for 2 minutes or until bright green and just tender. (If using broccoli flowerheads as well, add them after removing the stems and give them no more than 1 minute's boiling.) Drain in a colander, but save 125 ml (4 fl oz) of the liquid.

Heat the peanut oil in a wok and stir-fry the broccoli and the ginger for 1 minute. Add the oyster sauce, soy sauce, sugar, sesame oil and cooking liqiud, and let it boil up. Mix the cornflour with 15 ml (1 tbsp) of cold water and stir it into the liquid until it thickens slightly. Toss the broccoli pieces in the sauce and serve at once.

Serves 4
stems from a large bunch of broccoli
45 ml (3 tbsp) peanut oil
2.5 ml (½ tsp) grated fresh ginger
15 ml (1 tbsp) oyster sauce
15 ml (1 tbsp) light soy sauce
5 ml (1 tsp) sugar
2.5 ml (½ tsp) sesame oil
cooking liquid from blanching the broccoli
10 ml (2 tsp) cornflour

Peel any tough skin from broccoli stems.

Slice broccoli.

Stir-Fried Lettuce

Wash the lettuce, drain and dry well. Cut into halves lengthways, then cut each half twice lengthways and twice crossways to give chunky, bite-size pieces.

Heat a wok, add the peanut oil and swirl the wok to coat the inside with oil. Add the garlic and ginger and stir-fry for 10 seconds, then add the lettuce and stir-fry on high heat for 30 to 40 seconds. Turn off heat, add salt, sugar, soy sauce and sesame oil and toss to distribute the seasonings. The lettuce should retain its crisp texture. Serve at once, by itself or as a bed for other dishes.

Serves 4–6
1 firm lettuce
30–45 ml (2–3 tbsp) peanut oil
2.5 ml (½ tsp) crushed garlic
1.25 ml (¼ tsp) finely grated fresh ginger
1.25 ml (¼ tsp) salt
5 ml (1 tsp) sugar
10 ml (2 tsp) light soy sauce
few drops of sesame oil

Cut halved lettuce into chunky pieces.

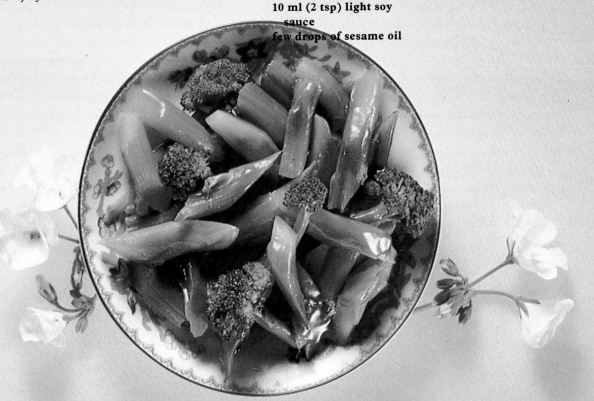

Braised Chinese Mushrooms and Bean Curd

Serves 4
8 dried Chinese
  mushrooms
225 g (8 oz) fried bean
  curd or pressed bean
  curd
45 ml (3 tbsp) peanut oil
2 spring onions, cut into
  5 cm (2 inch) lengths
175 ml (6 fl oz) stock
15 ml (1 tbsp) dark soy
  sauce
15 ml (1 tbsp) oyster sauce
2.5 ml (½ tsp) sugar
5 ml (1 tsp) cornflour
5 ml (1 tsp) sesame oil

There are two types of bean curd suitable for this dish – pressed bean curd and squares of fried bean curd – both are available from Chinese stores. The pressed bean curd will require deep frying before adding to the sauce.

Soak the mushrooms in water for 30 minutes. Drain, discard the mushroom stems and cut the caps in half.

Split squares of the fried bean curd into two, and then cut each square diagonally in half. If using the pressed bean curd, cut in the same way and then deep fry in hot oil until golden brown. Drain.

Heat a wok, add the peanut oil and swirl it around the wok. When hot, add the spring onions and mushrooms and stir on medium-high heat for about 30 seconds. Add the stock, soy sauce, oyster sauce, sugar and simmer, covered for 20 minutes. Add bean curd slices. Bring to the boil, cover the wok and simmer for 5 minutes.

Blend the cornflour with 15 ml (1 tbsp) of water and stir it into the sauce until it boils and thickens. Add sesame oil, toss the mixture lightly, and serve.

Note: The soft white bean curd (tofu) available in packets can be used for this dish but take care to avoid mashing it. Cook the spring onions and mushrooms, add the liquids and seasonings, then simmer and thicken as described. At that stage, open the container, slide the bean curd on to a plate and drain off its liquid. Cut it into squares and carefully slide it into the sauce over a low heat. Do not stir, but spoon some of the sauce over the bean curd to heat it through. Slide the mixture out of the wok on to a serving dish.

The pressed bean curd (left) and fried bean curd.

Remove stems and halve mushroom caps.

Split squares of bean curd, then cut diagonally in half.

Peppers with Pork and Prawns

Shell and de-vein the prawns; mince them finely. Combine them with the pork, salt, finely chopped spring onions and 10 ml (2 tsp) of the cornflour.

Cut the peppers lengthways into quarters; discard the seeds and membranes, and wash them well. Cut each quarter pepper across into half. Mound the minced mixture evenly on the pepper pieces.

Blend the remaining 5 ml (1 tsp) of cornflour with 15 ml (1 tbsp) of water. In a small bowl, combine the garlic, soy sauce, wine, bean sauce and sugar; mix in 90 ml (6 tbsp) of water.

Heat half the oil in a wok and fry half of the pepper pieces, meat side down. When the filling is brown, turn them over and cook for a further 2 minutes. Remove to a plate. Add the remaining oil to the wok and cook the remaining peppers. Remove.

Pour the garlic-liquid mixture into the wok, stir until boiling, then thicken it with the blended cornflour. Return the peppers and heat through. Scatter the matchstick strips of ham over the top, and serve.

Note: If the peppers are large, cut them into 12 pieces instead of 8 so that the end result will be a convenient, bite-sized portion.

Serves 6
225 g (8 oz) raw prawns
225 g (8 oz) minced pork
5 ml (1 tsp) salt
2 spring onions
15 ml (1 tbsp) cornflour
3 medium-sized red or green peppers
5 ml (1 tsp) crushed garlic
15 ml (1 tbsp) dark soy sauce
15 ml (1 tbsp) Chinese wine or dry sherry
15 ml (1 tbsp) bean sauce (Min Sze Jeung)
10 ml (2 tsp) sugar
75 ml (5 tbsp) oil
25 g (1 oz) lean ham, cut into matchstick strips

Cut each pepper into eight even-sized pieces.

Mound prawn and pork mixture on pepper.

Fry pepper, meat side down, then turn.

Stir-Fried Chinese Cabbage

Serves 4–6
**450 g (1 lb) Chinese chard
  cabbage (bok choy)**
**30–45 ml (2–3 tbsp) peanut
  oil**
**1 clove garlic, bruised
  (optional)**
3 slices fresh ginger
5 ml (1 tsp) sugar
5 ml (1 tsp) salt
5 ml (1 tsp) sesame oil

Prepare the Chinese cabbage. Separate the leaves from the heart, wash them well and trim off a small slice at their base. Lay the leaves flat on the chopping board and remove the tough leaf edges, leaving just a little border of green on the white stems. Cut the stems into 5 cm (2 inch) lengths.

Heat a wok, add the peanut oil and swirl to coat the wok. Add the garlic and ginger, and fry for a few seconds just until golden. Add the cabbage and stir-fry for 1 minute. Then add 50 ml (2 fl oz) water and the sugar and salt; cover the wok and simmer for 2 minutes.

Uncover and stir-fry again until most of the liquid evaporates. Turn off the heat, sprinkle the sesame oil over, and toss to distribute the oil. Remove and discard the garlic and ginger. Serve at once, with other dishes.
Note: If the cabbage is not being served right away or must be reheated, use a slightly different method. After washing and cutting the stems, blanch them in a large pan of lightly salted boiling water with 15 ml (1 tbsp) of oil added. Once the water returns to the boil, boil the cabbage for only 30 seconds, then drain. Just before serving stir-fry as above. This way the cabbage doesn't get that tired look if kept waiting.

Separate leaves of Chinese cabbage.

Remove the tough leaf edges.

To bruise garlic, hit firmly with chopper.

Shredded Gluten with Cashews

Serves 4
225 g (8 oz) prepared
  wheat gluten (see below)
225 g (8 oz) vegetables
60 ml (4 tbsp) peanut oil
2.5 ml (½ tsp) grated fresh
  ginger
2.5 ml (½ tsp) crushed
  garlic

15 ml (1 tbsp) bean sauce
2.5 ml (½ tsp) chilli sauce
  (optional)
15 ml (1 tbsp) light soy
  sauce
10 ml (2 tsp) cornflour
100 g (4 oz) deep fried
  cashew nuts

Shred the prepared gluten.

Choose a combination of two vegetables for this dish such as broccoli stems, red or green peppers, green beans, water chestnuts, bamboo shoots, spring onions.

Prepare the gluten and after it has been boiled and cooled, cut it into shreds. Cut the vegetables the same size as the gluten.

Heat a wok, add 45 ml (2 tbsp) of peanut oil and swirl to coat the inside of the wok. Cook the ginger and garlic over low heat for a few seconds. Then increase the heat, add the vegetables and stir-fry for a minute or two. Remove.

Add the remaining oil to the wok and stir-fry the gluten for 2 minutes. Mix the bean sauce, chilli and soy sauce with 125 ml (4 fl oz) water and stir it into the wok; cover the wok and simmer for 15 minutes.

Return the vegetables and cook for another 2 minutes. Blend cornflour with a little water, add and stir until the sauce boils and thickens. Add the cashews. Serve immediately with hot rice.

Gluten 'Steaks': In Oriental vegetarian diets we find soybeans in various forms, especially bean curd which the Chinese call 'the meat without a bone' because of its high protein value. Another way of introducing protein is with gluten 'steaks'. Gluten is the protein part of wheat and strong plain flour is high in gluten. The spongy steaks can be sliced or shredded as required and they absorb flavours readily.

Yields about 300 g (10 oz)
prepared gluten
75 g (3 oz) strong plain flour
125 ml (4 fl oz) water

Put the flour and water into a bowl and mix with a wooden spoon. It may be necessary to add a little more water, because the absorbency varies (as it does with plain flour). It will form a rubbery dough. With wet hands, shape the dough into a ball, place it in a bowl, cover and leave for 30 minutes.

Bring a large saucepan of water to the boil. On a wet board, cut the dough with a wet knife into slices 1.5 cm (¾ inch) thick. Drop them into the boiling water, cover the saucepan and cook for 30 minutes. They will swell to about three times their size.

Drain in a colander and allow to cool. When cool enough to handle, squeeze gently to remove excess water. Refrigerate, covered with plastic wrap. They will keep for up to a week.

Pickled Mustard Cabbage

Put the sugar, water, salt and vinegar into a saucepan and stir over heat until the sugar dissolves. Bring to the boil and simmer for 5 minutes. Leave to cool completely.

Using only the stem and leaf ribs of the well-washed mustard cabbage, cut into chunks 2.5 cm (1 inch) long. After trimming there should be 225 g (8 oz). (The leaves may be shredded and used in soup or other dishes.)

Bring a large saucepan of water to the boil and blanch the mustard cabbage chunks for 1 minute. Drain, and cool under running cold water.

Rinse out a large glass jar with hot water, put in the mustard cabbage and ginger. Top up with the spiced vinegar mixture, cover and refrigerate for 3 to 4 days before using.

This crisp pickled vegetable makes a refreshing snack, and the flavour is enhanced when eaten with a little sesame oil.

225 g cup (8 oz) sugar
700 ml (1¼ pints) water
15 ml (1 tbsp) salt
150 ml (¼ pint) cider vinegar
1 bunch 450 g (1 lb) Chinese mustard cabbage (gai choy)
4 slices of fresh ginger

The mustard cabbage.

Drain and cool the blanched cabbage.

Pickled Vegetables

1 small white turnip
½ cucumber
½ carrot
10 slices fresh ginger
1 red chilli, diced
1 red pepper, diced
20 ml (4 tsp) salt
75 ml (5 tbsp) sugar
75 ml (5 tbsp) cider vinegar

Cut the turnip, cucumber and carrot into bite-sized pieces. Add the ginger slices, red chilli, red pepper and salt. Mix well, and leave to stand for 6 hours.

Lightly rinse the vegetables, drain, then return them to a bowl. Add sugar and vinegar, mix well and allow to stand for 6 hours in the refrigerator.

Note: The ingredients may be diced, shredded or diagonally cross-cut into big or little pieces according to your preference, and the soaking time should be adjusted accordingly.

Cut vegetables into bite-sized pieces.

Add ginger, chilli, pepper and salt to vegetables.

Szechwan-Style Aubergine

Slice off and discard the stalk end of the aubergines, but do not peel them. Cut in half lengthways, then into wedges lengthways each about 2.5 cm (1 inch) thick. Cut the wedges into 5 cm (2 inch) lengths.

Heat the peanut oil in a wok or frying pan, and fry half of the pieces of aubergine at a time on high heat, turning the pieces so that they are evenly browned. Let them cook to a dark golden brown, then lift them out with a slotted spoon and drain on absorbent kitchen paper. When all the aubergine pieces have been fried, set them aside to cool. The oil that remains may be strained and used again.

Combine the sauce ingredients and stir until sugar dissolves.

Pour off all but 15 ml (1 tbsp) of oil remaining in the pan. Heat, then add the ginger and garlic and stir quickly over medium heat until they turn golden.

Add the sauce mixture, bring to the boil, then return the aubergine and cook over high heat, turning the aubergine pieces over until most of the sauce is absorbed. Transfer to a serving dish as soon as cooking is completed (don't leave aubergine in the wok or a metallic taste will develop). Serve warm or cold.

Serves 6
2 aubergines about 450 g
  (1 lb) each, or 900 g
  (2 lb) smaller
  aubergines
450 ml (¾ pint) peanut oil
5 ml (1 tsp) finely grated
  ginger
5 ml (1 tsp) finely chopped
  garlic
Sauce:
75 ml (5 tbsp) dark soy
  sauce
20 ml (4 tsp) vinegar
20 ml (4 tsp) Chinese wine
  or dry sherry
30 ml (2 tbsp) sugar
5 ml (1 tsp) sesame oil
5 ml (1 tsp) chilli oil
  (optional)
5–10 ml (1–2 tsp) sweet
  chilli sauce

Cut wedges of aubergine into lengths.

Deep-fry aubergine in two lots until brown, then drain.

Stir-Fried Watercress with Bean Curd

Serves 4
450 g (1 lb) watercress
5 ml (1 tsp) salt
30 ml (2 tbsp) peanut oil
1 large dried red chilli
2.5 ml (½ tsp) crushed garlic
10 ml (2 tsp) sesame oil
225 g (8 oz) fresh bean curd
Sauce:
20 ml (4 tsp) light soy sauce
20 ml (4 tsp) Chinese wine or dry sherry
2.5 ml (½ tsp) sesame oil
5 ml (1 tsp) chopped fresh coriander leaves

Wash the watercress well and shake dry. Finely chop the leaves and stems, place in a bowl, sprinkle with the salt and toss well. Cover the bowl and chill for 30 minutes or longer. Drain and squeeze out liquid.

Heat a wok over a medium heat, add the peanut oil and when hot, add the whole chilli and fry until it is dark in colour. On high heat fry the garlic for just 3 or 4 seconds; add the watercress and stir-fry, turning constantly for 30 seconds. Turn off the heat, mix in the sesame oil and turn the mixture out into a serving dish. Allow to cool, and chill.

Have the bean curd well chilled. Combine the ingredients for the sauce in a small serving bowl. Drain the bean curd, cut it into squares and carefully place them on the chilled watercress. Sprinkle the sauce over the dish.

Finely chop leaves and stems of washed watercress.

A whole chilli is fried in the oil for flavour.

Carefully cut the drained bean curd into slices.

Vegetable Platter with Sesame Sauce

Serves 6
25 g (1 oz) agar-agar
225 g (8 oz) button
mushrooms
30 ml (2 tbsp) peanut oil
salt to taste
225 g (8 oz) green beans
4 spring onions
225 g (8 oz) bean curd
1 carrot
Sesame Sauce:
60 ml (4 tbsp) bottled
sesame sauce
20 ml (4 tsp) light soy
sauce
20 ml (4 tsp) water
20 ml (4 tsp) sesame oil
2.5 ml (½ tsp) chilli oil

This cold vegetable platter makes an ideal hors d'oeuvre or a light meal. Other suitable vegetables are cooked asparagus, blanched broccoli stems, sliced (canned) water chestnuts, strips of courgettes that have been briefly fried in a little oil, and cold cooked egg noodles.

Soak the agar-agar in cold water for 10 minutes; then drain and cut into 5 cm (2 inch) lengths. Wipe the mushrooms with a damp towel, discard their stems and slice the caps.

Heat a wok, add the peanut oil and heat. Add the mushrooms and stir-fry over a moderate heat for 2 minutes. Turn out on to a serving dish and season to taste with salt. Allow to cool.

String the beans, removing ends; leave whole, or halve if large. Blanch the beans in boiling water for 3 minutes, then drain and cool. Cut the spring onions into bite-size lengths. Slice the bean curd. Peel the carrot and cut it into strips. Blanch briefly – they should still be crisp.

Arrange the vegetables on a serving platter, with a bowl of the sauce for spooning over them.
Sesame Sauce: Stir the sesame sauce until it is smooth, then blend in the other ingredients. In cold weather it may be necessary to warm the sesame sauce before mixing.

The dried and soaked agar-agar.

Slice mushroom caps.

Stir-Fried Eggs with Mixed Vegetables

Serves 4–6
4 eggs
2.5 ml (½ tsp) salt
15 g (1 oz) dried wood
   fungus (cloud ears)
225 g (8 oz) Chinese
   cabbage
1 carrot
4 spring onions
30 ml (2 tbsp) peanut oil
2.5 ml (½ tsp) finely
   grated fresh ginger
15 ml (1 tbsp) light soy
   sauce
2.5 ml (½ tsp) sugar
5 ml (1 tsp) sesame oil

Wood fungus is a texture ingredient which looks rather pretty when it is soaked and swells into shapes like billowing storm clouds. It is also known as cloud ear fungus or wun yee.

Beat the eggs with salt until yolks and whites are mixed.

Soak the wood fungus in a large bowl of water for 15 minutes. Then rinse well and trim off any gritty portions. Cut large pieces in half.

Cut cabbage leaves in half lengthways (or thirds if they are large), then shred finely crossways. This keeps the shreds from being long and stringy. Cut the carrot into matchstick strips. Cut the spring onions into short lengths.

Heat a wok, add 15 ml (1 tbsp) of the peanut oil and stir-fry the eggs until they set. Remove to a plate.

Wipe out the wok. Add the remaining 15 ml (1 tbsp) of peanut oil and when hot, fry the ginger for a few seconds. Add the cabbage and carrot, and stir-fry for 1 minute, then cover the wok and cook until half tender (about 2 minutes). Add the spring onions, wood fungus, soy sauce, sugar and sesame oil. Stir to mix, cover the wok and cook on low heat for 1 minute. Add the cooked eggs, toss well together, and serve immediately.

Finely shred the cabbage.

Stir-fry beaten eggs until they set.

Add spring onions and wood fungus to vegetables in wok.

Stir-Fried Salad Sprouts

Serves 4
**225 g (8 oz) bean or lentil
  sprouts or alfalfa**
1 large carrot
2 spring onions
**stalks of choy sum
  (Chinese greens,
  optional)**
15 ml (1 tbsp) peanut oil
**2.5 ml (½ tsp) finely
  chopped garlic**
**15 ml (1 tbsp) light soy
  sauce**
15 ml (1 tbsp) oyster sauce
few drops of sesame oil

Rinse the salad sprouts in a large bowl of cold water. Drain well in a colander. Pinch off straggly tails of the bean sprouts if time permits.

Cut the carrot into long diagonal slices no more than 6 mm (¼ inch) thick; then stack three or four slices together and cut into matchstick strips. Either blanch the carrot strips in boiling water for 1 minute; or if you have a microwave cooker, cover them with plastic wrap and microwave for 30 seconds.

Cut the lower half of the spring onions into bite-size lengths; roughly chop the dark green leaves (keep the two separate). If using choy sum, cut into bite-size lengths.

Place a wok over heat and when hot, pour in the peanut oil and allow to heat, then swirl the wok so that it is coated with oil. Throw in the garlic and spring onion leaves, and stir-fry for 30 seconds. Add the choy sum, and stir-fry for 1 minute. Add the well-drained sprouts, white portion of spring onion and carrot, and stir-fry for 1 minute. Then add the soy sauce and oyster sauce, and mix well. Turn off the heat, sprinkle the sesame oil over, toss to mix, and serve at once.

Note: If liked, bean curd (cut into strips or dice) may be added with the sprouts. In a vegetarian diet, this provides protein.

Rinse and drain the combined sprouts.

Cut carrots into matchstick strips.

Chop tops of spring onions and cut white part into lengths.

Braised Gluten with Vegetables

Thinly slice the gluten.

Discard any hard bits from soaked wood fungus.

Add mushroom liquid and flavourings to fried gluten.

Prepare the gluten and after it has been boiled and cooled, cut it into thin slices.

Soak the mushrooms in 350 ml (12 fl oz) hot water for 20 minutes. Drain (reserving the water), discard the mushroom stems and cut the caps into slices. Soak the wood fungus in cold water for 10 minutes; drain, discard any hard bits and cut into bite-size pieces.

Cut the carrot into matchstick strips. Cut the beans into diagonal slices. Chop the spring onions and put them on a saucer with the grated ginger.

Heat a wok, add the peanut oil and swirl to coat the wok. Fry the spring onions and ginger for a few seconds; then add the sliced gluten and mushrooms and fry for a minute or two. Add 250 ml (8 fl oz) of the mushroom soaking liquid and stir in the soy sauces, sugar and 10 ml (2 tsp) of the sesame oil. Cover and simmer on low heat for 8 minutes.

Add the carrots and beans, cover the wok and simmer for a further 8 minutes.

Finally, stir the wood fungus through and cook for 2 minutes longer. The liquid in the wok should now be reduced to about 50 ml (2 fl oz). Sprinkle with the remaining 5 ml (1 tsp) of sesame oil, and serve at once.

Serves 4

225 g (8 oz) prepared gluten (see page 53)

6 dried Chinese mushrooms

30 ml (2 tbsp) dried wood fungus (cloud ears)

1 carrot

12 green beans

3 spring onions

5 ml (1 tsp) finely grated ginger

30 ml (2 tbsp) peanut oil

15 ml (1 tbsp) light soy sauce

15 ml (1 tbsp) dark soy sauce

10 ml (2 tsp) sugar

15 ml (1 tbsp) sesame oil

Bean Curd with Hot Sauce

Cut the bean curd into small dice. Have the chopped ginger, garlic and spring onion ready on a plate. Bring 1 litre of water to a rolling boil in a wok, add the diced bean curd and bring the water back to the boil for a few minutes until the bean curd is heated through. Pour into a sieve and allow to drain.

Dry off the wok, add the peanut oil and when hot, stir-fry the ginger, garlic and spring onion.

Add the stock (or water), bean sauce, chilli paste, tomato sauce, salt, sugar and soy sauce; allow it to boil. Blend the cornflour with 15 ml (1 tbsp) of cold water, and stir it into the mixture.

Place the bean curd in the wok, and sprinkle the sesame oil over. With a large ladle, scoop the sauce over it – taking care not to mash the bean curd. If liked serve on a bed of Stir-Fried Lettuce (see page 49) and garnish with a chilli flower.

Cut bean curd into dice.

Scoop sauce over bean curd.

Serves 4

**4 squares pressed bean curd
5 ml (1 tsp) finely chopped fresh ginger
5 ml (1 tsp) finely chopped garlic
15 ml (1 tbsp) finely chopped spring onion
15 ml (1 tbsp) peanut oil
125 ml (4 fl oz) stock or water
5 ml (1 tsp) ground bean sauce (mor sze jeung)
5 ml (1 tsp) chilli paste
15 ml (1 tbsp) tomato sauce
2.5 ml (½ tsp) salt
2.5 ml (½ tsp) sugar
5 ml (1 tsp) dark soy sauce
5 ml (1 tsp) cornflour
drops of sesame oil**

Braised Bitter Melon

Serves 4–6

3 medium-sized bitter
melons
350 g (12 oz) minced pork,
or raw prawns
30 ml (2 tbsp) finely
chopped spring onions
5 ml (1 tsp) finely grated
fresh ginger
2.5 ml (½ tsp) crushed
garlic
2.5 ml (½ tsp) salt
1 egg, beaten
15 ml (1 tbsp) cornflour
15 ml (1 tbsp) canned
salted black beans
5 ml (1 tsp) finely chopped
garlic
75 ml (5 tbsp) peanut oil
15 ml (1 tbsp) sesame oil
Sauce
125 ml (4 fl oz) stock or
water
15 ml (1 tbsp) light soy
sauce
5 ml (1 tsp) sugar

Cut each bitter melon crossways into 4 cm (1½ inch)
slices, discarding stem end and pointed tip. With a sharp
knife, remove and discard the spongy centre and seeds,
leaving tubular sections.

Mix pork or prawns with ginger, crushed garlic, salt,
30 ml (2 tbsp) of the beaten egg and 10 ml (2 tsp) of the
cornflour, combining thoroughly. Fill the sections of
melon with this mixture, mounding the filling slightly on
one side.

Rinse the black beans in a strainer under cold water,
drain well, and mash the beans with a fork or chop finely.
Mix with the finely chopped garlic. In a separate bowl,
mix the sauce ingredients together.

Heat a wok, add the peanut oil and swirl to coat. Put
the pieces of melon into the wok and fry on medium heat
just until the filling starts to brown. This may be done in
batches. Lift out on a slotted spoon and set aside on a
plate.

Pour off all but 15 ml (1 tbsp) of oil, add the black
beans-garlic mixture and fry, stirring, for 1 minute. Add
the sauce ingredients mixed together and bring to the
boil. Return slices of melon to the wok with the rounded
side upwards. Cover the wok and simmer on low heat for
15 to 20 minutes.

Remove the melon pieces to a serving plate. Mix the
remaining cornflour with 15 ml (1 tbsp) of cold water,
add it to the sauce in the wok and stir until it thickens.
Drizzle in the remaining beaten egg, stirring as it sets.
Turn off heat and stir in sesame oil. Pour over the melon
and serve with rice.

*Remove spongy centre from
thick slices of bitter melon.*

*Fill bitter melon with pork
mixture.*

*Fry pieces of melon until
filling begins to brown.*

Stir-Fried Runner Beans and Minced Pork

Serves 4–6

450 g (1 lb) runner beans
60 ml (4 tbsp) peanut oil
15 ml (1 tbsp) finely
grated fresh ginger
225 g (8 oz) minced pork
60 ml (4 tbsp) roughly
chopped spring onions
Sauce:
125 ml (4 fl oz) chicken
stock
15 ml (1 tbsp) light soy
sauce
10 ml (2 tsp) oyster sauce
5 ml (1 tsp) cornflour

Top and tail the runner beans, wash and pat dry on paper towels. Cut into 5 cm (2 inch) lengths and set aside.

Mix the sauce ingredients except for cornflour; set aside. Separately, mix the cornflour with 15 ml (1 tbsp) of cold water; set this aside as well.

Heat a wok, add 45 ml (3 tbsp) of the oil and swirl. Fry 5 ml (1 tsp) of the ginger for 10 seconds, then add the beans and stir-fry for 1 minute. Remove to a plate.

Return the wok to the heat, add the remaining 15 ml (1 tbsp) of oil and when hot, add the remaining 10 ml (2 tsp) of ginger, fry for a few seconds, then add the pork and stir-fry on high heat until its colour changes. Keep tossing, and press against the hot wok with back of frying spoon so that it is all well cooked.

Add the sauce ingredients and the beans, stir, cover, and cook for 3 minutes. Uncover, add spring onions and toss over high heat. Stir in the cornflour-water paste until the sauce thickens. Serve immediately.

Cut runner beans into lengths.

Stir-fry pork until colour changes.

Seafood

The Chinese have a way with seafood, choosing only the freshest and best, then cooking it to perfection. The prime rule is never to overcook delicate fish or shellfish. Watch carefully and be guided by the cooking times even if they seem improbably short.

Fish must be purchased as fresh as possible, with bright clear eyes, light red gills and firm flesh, smelling sweetly of the sea. Prawns should be sweet smelling, firm and springy, not limp and soft when pressed, not dark around the head.

For best results, lobsters and crabs must be purchased live. (Once dead, the flesh spoils quickly.) In most areas these are only available boiled, and as Chinese recipes require them not to be pre-cooked, this poses a problem.

My Chinese mentor, a top-flight cook and restaurateur, has demonstrated for me how he despatches the lobster with one quick swipe of the chopper aimed where head and body meet. This may be the quickest way to kill it, but most people (including me) have neither the nerve nor the heart to cut up a live creature.

There has been much controversy about the most humane way to deal with crustaceans, and I have read what many leading cookery authorities have written on the subject. I suggest putting it in the deep freeze for an hour or so to send it quietly to sleep. Another method is to drop the creature head first into boiling water; this kills it very quickly. One method was to use merely hot water, but it was argued that this was a slow death and that boiling water was preferable. After about a minute when it has stopped moving, remove it from the water. This is not sufficient to cook the flesh and no flavour will be lost. Then proceed as in the recipe.

Left: clockwise from front: raw prawns; steamed scallops in shells; flounder; scallops; 2 whiting; crayfish; perch; bream; crabs; trout; crab; cooked prawns.

Fried Fish with Chilli Bean Sauce

Scale and clean the fish thoroughly, leaving head and tail on. Trim off any spines with kitchen scissors. Wash fish well and dry on paper towels. With a sharp knife or chopper, score the fish lengthways, making parallel cuts about a finger's width apart and almost through to the bone to allow seasonings to penetrate.

Combine 45 ml (3 tbsp) of the wine with the light soy sauce, and marinate the fish in this mixture, making sure it goes into all the cuts.

Drain the marinade from the fish. Heat a wok, add the peanut oil and when very hot, add the fish. Deep-fry for 3 to 4 minutes on each side until both fish are brown and cooked. Turn the fish once only when cooking. Drain on a slotted spoon and place the fish on a heated serving platter.

Pour off most of the oil from the wok but leave about 60 ml (4 tbsp). Stir-fry the ginger and garlic over medium heat until the garlic starts to turn golden. Add the bean sauce, and stir; then add 250 ml (8 fl oz) water.

Mix the sauce ingredients with the remaining wine, add this to the wok and stir constantly until the mixture comes to the boil and thickens slightly. Finely chop the spring onions and stir them in. Pour the sauce over the fish and serve with rice.

Score fish lengthways.

Deep fry fish, turning once.

Serves 4

2 whole firm white fish, about 700 g (1½ lb) each – red mullet, sole or trout

75 ml (5 tbsp) Chinese wine or dry sherry

30 ml (2 tbsp) light soy sauce

peanut oil for frying

15 ml (1 tbsp) finely grated fresh ginger

10 ml (2 tsp) crushed garlic

30 ml (2 tbsp) hot bean sauce

4 spring onions

Sauce:

10 ml (2 tsp) cornflour

5 ml (1 tsp) sugar

30 ml (2 tbsp) dark soy sauce

Fried Mountain Trout with Ginger

Clean the cavity of the trout with damp absorbent kitchen paper dipped in salt. Make shallow diagonal cuts on the fish and rub in salt and five spice powder mixed together. Roll the fish in cornflour to coat it and dust off any excess.

Cut the spring onions in bite-size pieces. Combine the sauce ingredients.

Heat a wok, add the peanut oil and when very hot, fry the ginger and spring onions for just a few seconds until they are soft but not brown. Remove on a frying spoon and set aside on a plate. Place the fish in the wok, and fry until they are golden brown underneath; then turn them over, lower the heat and fry until the other side is browned too and the fish are cooked through.

Pour off as much oil as possible. Pour the sauce mixture over the fish. Return the ginger and spring onions, raise the heat and cook for 1 minute or until the sauce boils. Lift the fish on to a warm serving dish, spoon the sauce over, and serve garnished with coriander and carrots.

Note: Young tender ginger, which has translucent skin and pink tips, is best for this dish. If this is not available, reduce the quantity of ginger by half.

Serves 4

4 trout, about 175 g (6 oz) each
5 ml (1 tsp) salt
2.5 ml (½ tsp) five spice powder
60 ml (4 tbsp) cornflour
3 spring onions
120 ml (8 tbsp) peanut oil
30 ml (2 tbsp) very finely shredded fresh young ginger
Sauce:
30 ml (2 tbsp) Chinese red vinegar or wine vinegar
30 ml (2 tbsp) Chinese wine or sherry
60 ml (4 tbsp) light soy sauce
10 ml (2 tsp) sugar
10 ml (2 tsp) sesame oil
30 ml (2 tbsp) chopped fresh coriander

Finely shred young ginger.

Fry the fish in wok, turning once.

Return ginger and spring onion to fish and sauce.

Crisp-Skin Fish with Mushroom Sauce

Serves 4–6

1 whole fish, about 1.5 kg (3 lb) – snapper or other firm white fish

flour, seasoned with salt

oil for frying

1 large lemon for garnishing

Mushroom Sauce:

6 dried Chinese mushrooms

120 ml (8 tbsp) vinegar

120 ml (8 tbsp) sugar

30 ml (2 tbsp) light soy sauce

30 ml (2 tbsp) finely chopped spring onion

15 ml (1 tbsp) cornflour

30 ml (2 tbsp) preserved cucumber slices in syrup (optional)

Buy the fish cleaned and scaled, but with the head left on. Trim the fins and tail with kitchen scissors, and wipe out the cavity with absorbent paper dipped in coarse salt. Wash well and dry thoroughly. With a sharp knife, slash the fish diagonally on each side almost to the centre bone, forming diamond shapes in the flesh. Set the fish aside while you make the sauce.

Mushroom Sauce: Soak the mushrooms in hot water for 30 minutes. Drain, discard the mushroom stems and slice the caps finely. Put the mushrooms, vinegar, sugar and soy sauce into a small saucepan; add 175 ml (6 fl oz) water, and boil for 5 minutes. Add the spring onion. Add the cornflour blended with 15 ml (1 tbsp) of cold water and cook, stirring, until the sauce is clear and thickened. Remove from heat and keep warm. Stir in the preserved cucumber.

Dip the fish in seasoned flour, shaking off excess. Deep fry the fish in hot oil until golden brown. Drain it on a wire spoon and transfer it to a serving dish. Spoon the sauce over and garnish with lemon butterflies. This fish is good hot or cold.

Score the fish into a diamond pattern.

Add preserved cucumber to sauce.

Fish Braised in Soy Sauce

Serves 4–6

1 whole snapper, about 1.5 kg (3 lb)

5 ml (1 tsp) salt

30 ml (2 tbsp) cornflour

5 ml (1 tsp) five spice powder

2 spring onions

120 ml (8 tbsp) peanut oil

6 thin slices fresh ginger

2 cloves garlic, bruised

1 whole star anise

Sauce:

75 ml (5 tbsp) dark soy sauce

30 ml (2 tbsp) dry sherry

10 ml (2 tsp) sesame oil

15 ml (1 tbsp) sugar

Wash and clean the fish, leaving the head on. Wipe dry with absorbent kitchen paper. Score the fish lightly, no more than half-way to the bone, making three or four diagonal slashes on each side. Combine salt, cornflour and five spice powder; rub this mixture over the fish to coat it lightly, dust off excess.

Cut the spring onions into short lengths. In a bowl, combine the sauce ingredients with 125 ml (4 fl oz) water, and stir until the sugar dissolves.

Heat a wok, add the peanut oil and when very hot, slide the fish very carefully into the oil; fry over high heat for 2 minutes or until the underside of the fish is golden brown. Turn the fish, using a large spatula under the thickest part of the fish and helping it with a second spatula. Cook on the second side for a further 2 minutes or until golden.

Pour off the oil. Add the sauce mixture, pouring it over the fish. Add the spring onions, ginger, garlic and star anise. Reduce the heat so that the liquid simmers gently; cover the wok and cook for 10 to 12 minutes, basting two or three times with the sauce. Test at thickest part of fish with point of knife – if the flesh is milky white and flakes easily, the fish is cooked.

Carefully lift fish on to serving plate and spoon some sauce over it.

Rub salt, cornflour, and five spice powder into the scored fish.

Add spring onions, ginger, garlic and star anise to fish in wok.

Braised Rainbow Trout in Piquant Sauce

Score fish on both sides.

Fry fish in hot oil.

Simmer fish in sauce.

Serves 4–6
1 rainbow trout, about 900 g (2 lb)
30 ml (2 tbsp) cornflour
5 ml (1 tsp) salt
1.25 ml (¼ tsp) five spice powder
250 ml (8 fl oz) oil
2 spring onions, coarsely chopped
10 ml (2 tsp) finely chopped fresh ginger
Sauce:
30 ml (2 tbsp) dry sherry
30 ml (2 tbsp) light soy sauce
10 ml (2 tsp) sugar
10 ml (2 tsp) cider vinegar
5 ml (1 tsp) sesame oil
Garnish:
45 ml (3 tbsp) chopped fresh coriander leaves

Wipe the fish and make deep diagonal cuts on both sides. Combine the cornflour, salt and five spice powder, mixing thoroughly. Sprinkle the trout with this mixture, rubbing it well into the slashes, then dust off the excess.

In a bowl, combine the sauce ingredients; add 125 ml (4 fl oz) water, and stir until the sugar is dissolved.

Heat a wok, add the oil and when hot, slide the fish into the oil and fry on medium heat for 2 minutes until browned on one side; then turn it over and fry the other side for 2 minutes. Remove the fish from the wok.

Pour off all but 15 ml (1 tbsp) of the oil. When this is very hot, stir-fry the spring onions and ginger for 1 minute; they should not brown. Add the mixed sauce ingredients to the wok and bring to the boil. Return the fish and let it simmer, covered, and on low heat for 5 minutes. Carefully turn the fish over and let it simmer for a further 4 to 5 minutes.

Lift the fish onto a warmed serving dish. The cornflour coating on the fish may have been sufficient to slightly thicken the sauce. If not, mix 5 ml (1 tsp) of cornflour with 5 ml (1 tsp) of cold water, stir this into the sauce and allow it to boil up and thicken. Spoon the sauce over the fish, sprinkle liberally with chopped coriander.

Steamed Whole Fish with Mushrooms and Ham

Serves 6–8

1 whole fish, about 2 kg
  (4 lb) – snapper or
  salmon trout
2.5 ml (½ tsp) salt
5 ml (1 tsp) ginger juice
6 dried Chinese
  mushrooms
15 ml (1 tbsp) light soy
  sauce
10 ml (2 tsp) sugar
5 ml (1 tsp) sesame oil

15 ml (1 tbsp) Chinese
  wine or dry sherry
50 g (2 oz) ham
2 spring onions
15 ml (1 tbsp) finely
  grated fresh ginger
Dipping Sauces:
light soy sauce
grated ginger soaked in
  60 ml (4 tbsp) sherry
sesame oil
chilli oil

How to deal with a fish too large to fit into your bamboo steamer.

Wash and clean the fish, wipe with paper towels. Score the fish six times on one side, cutting diagonally into the flesh down to the bone. Rub the fish inside and out with salt and ginger juice, rubbing into the scorings. Set aside.

Soak the mushrooms in hot water for 30 minutes. Drain, but reserve 75 ml (5 tbsp) of the water; discard the mushroom stems and slice the caps thinly. Put the mushrooms in a small pan; add the soy sauce, sugar and the 75 ml (5 tbsp) of mushroom soaking water. Bring to the boil, then cover the pan and simmer for 10 minutes. Lift out the mushrooms and set them aside. Add the sesame oil and wine to the liquid left in the pan.

Cut the ham and spring onions into strips. Lightly oil a heatproof dish and place half the ginger, ham and spring onions on the dish. Place the fish on these, uncut side down. Place the mushrooms and the remaining ginger, ham and spring onions in the scorings of fish. Pour the liquid in the pan over the top.

Set a wire rack in a large baking dish and pour in boiling water to a depth of 1.3 cm (½ inch). Place the dish containing the fish on the rack, cover all with a large sheet of aluminium foil, folding the foil over the rim of the baking dish. Place the baking dish on top of the stove and have the heat medium-high so that there is a lot of steam. Cook the fish for about 20 minutes. Remove foil.

Serve with small bowls for the dipping sauces, so that each diner can make his or her own mixture. If liked, garnish with sprigs of fresh coriander or spring onion curls.

Place vegetables and ham into fish scorings.

Place prepared fish on rack.

Chilli Shrimp and Bamboo Shoot

This highly seasoned mixture, which flavours the bland bean starch (transparent) noodles, is typical of the hot inland provinces of China.

Soak the dried shrimps in hot water for 30 minutes. Drain well and pat dry with paper towels; pulverise in an electric blender and set aside. Chop the bamboo shoot and set aside.

Separate approximately 50 g (2 oz) bean starch noodles using kitchen shears, place in a pan of boiling water and boil for 15 minutes. Drain and set aside.

Heat a wok, add the peanut oil and swirl to coat the sides of the wok. When hot add the garlic, ginger, powdered shrimp and bamboo shoot; stir-fry for 1 minute. Then add sauce ingredients mixed together, stirring until it boils and thickens. Add sesame oil, stir, and garnish with chopped spring onions.

Place the drained bean starch noodles on a serving dish, and spoon the shrimp mixture over them. Serve immediately.

Serves 4
75 ml (5 tbsp) dried
  shrimps
50 g (2 oz) bean starch
  noodles
225 g (8 oz) canned winter
  bamboo shoot
30 ml (2 tbsp) peanut oil
2.5 ml (½ tsp) finely
  chopped garlic
2.5 ml (½ tsp) finely
  chopped fresh ginger
few drops of sesame oil
30 ml (2 tbsp) chopped
  spring onions
Sauce:
10 ml (2 tsp) dark soy
  sauce
2.5 ml (½ tsp) salt
5 ml (1 tsp) sugar
125 ml (4 fl oz) chicken
  stock
10 ml (2 tsp) chilli oil
5 ml (1 tsp) cornflour

Chop the bamboo shoot.

Drain boiled bean starch noodles.

Add sauce to the stir-fried mixture.

Layered Seafood with Oyster Sauce

Remove the skin and any small bones from the fish fillets. Slit the prawns along the curve of the back and remove the sandy vein. Finely chop the prawns and put into a bowl with the ginger, chopped spring onions, water chestnuts, salt, cornflour and sesame oil. Mix together thoroughly.

Spread the mixture on the fillets of fish with a spatula or table knife, then use a chopper to cut the fish into pieces of convenient size.

Divide the broccoli into florets and slice the broccoli stems thinly. Cut the spring onions into 2.5 cm (1 inch) lengths. Mix together all the sauce ingredients except the cornflour.

Heat about 700 ml (1¼ pints) peanut oil in a wok and when hot, add the pieces of fish (not too many at a time), prawn side downwards. Fry until golden. Remove to absorbent kitchen paper to drain, then arrange on a serving dish and keep warm.

When all the fish has been fried, pour off the oil, leaving about 15 ml (1 tbsp). Reheat the oil, add the spring onions and crushed garlic, and stir-fry for 10 seconds. Add the broccoli and fry for a few seconds longer. Then pour in the sauce mixture, bring to the boil, cover the wok and cook for 2 minutes.

Mix the 15 ml (1 tbsp) of cornflour with 15 ml (1 tbsp) of cold water, stir this into the sauce until it boils and thickens. Remove from heat. Arrange the broccoli around the fish, then spoon the sauce over, and serve.

Serves 6
450 g (1 lb) haddock fillets
225 g (8 oz) shelled raw
  prawns
2.5 ml (½ tsp) finely
  grated fresh ginger
60 ml (4 tbsp) finely
  chopped spring onion
45 ml (3 tbsp) finely
  chopped water
  chestnuts
5 ml (1 tsp) salt
5 ml (1 tsp) cornflour
5 ml (1 tsp) sesame oil
1 bunch broccoli
additional 2 spring onions
peanut oil for deep frying
2.5 ml (½ tsp) crushed
  garlic
Sauce:
20 ml (4 tsp) oyster sauce
250 ml (8 fl oz) chicken
  stock
20 ml (4 tsp) Chinese wine
  or dry sherry
5 ml (1 tsp) white vinegar
2.5 ml (½ tsp) sugar
15 ml (1 tbsp) cornflour

Spread prawn mixture on fish fillets.

Fry fish pieces until golden.

Stir-fry broccoli with spring onion and garlic.

Prawn and Bean Curd Puffs in Oyster Sauce

Drain liquid from bean curd.

Stir bean curd into prawn mixture.

Deep fry mixture until golden.

Serves 4

225 g (8 oz) raw prawns
2.5 ml (¼ tsp) salt
15 ml (1 tbsp) cornflour
1 egg
2.5 ml (½ tsp) grated fresh
    ginger
2.5 ml (½ tsp) sesame oil
225 g (8 oz) fresh bean
    curd
oil for deep frying
Sauce:
175 ml (6 fl oz) chicken
    stock or water
15 ml (1 tbsp) oyster sauce
1 spring onion, chopped
15 ml (1 tbsp) chopped
    fresh coriander
10 ml (2 tsp) cornflour

Shell and de-vein the prawns. Put them into a food processor with salt, cornflour, egg, ginger and sesame oil; process until all ingredients are minced and the mixture is smooth. Alternatively, the prawns can be chopped very finely and combined with the other ingredients.

Drain the liquid from bean curd and pat dry with absorbent kitchen paper. Add the prawn mixture and stir well together with a fork to mix.

Combine the sauce ingredients except cornflour in a small saucepan, and heat to boiling. Blend the cornflour with 15 ml (1 tbsp) of cold water and stir it into the sauce until it boils and thickens.

Heat a wok, add enough oil for deep frying and fry spoonfuls of the prawn mixture until they are puffy and golden brown all over. This will have to be done in four or five batches. Drain them well, place on a serving dish and pour the hot sauce over. Serve immediately.

Shrimp with Asparagus and Cloud Ears

Serves 4

450 g (1 lb) raw shrimps (or prawns)

5 ml (1 tsp) crushed garlic

5 ml (1 tsp) finely grated fresh ginger

45 ml (3 tbsp) dried wood fungus (cloud ears)

1 bundle tender asparagus

1 medium-sized onion

75 ml (5 tbsp) peanut oil

Sauce:

45 ml (3 tbsp) light soy sauce

45 ml (3 tbsp) Chinese wine or dry sherry

45 ml (3 tbsp) Oriental sweet chilli sauce

10 ml (2 tsp) sesame oil

5 ml (1 tsp) cornflour

Cloud ears, or wood fungus, is a texture ingredient. Having no flavour of its own, it needs to be combined with a robust sauce.

Shell the shrimps and de-vein them if necessary. Rinse in cold water and dry on absorbent kitchen paper. Rub the garlic and ginger over the shrimps and set aside.

Soak the wood fungus in water for 10 minutes. Rinse well and trim away any gritty portions. Leave soaking in fresh cold water until required (but drain before use).

Wash the asparagus thoroughly and trim off any tough ends. If necessary, peel the bottom half of each stalk. Cut into bite-size pieces, keeping the tips whole. Peel the onion, cut in half lengthways, then cut each half into six wedge-shaped sections. Mix the sauce ingredients.

Heat a wok and when very hot, add 45 ml (3 tbsp) of the peanut oil and heat again, swirling to coat the wok. Add the shrimps and stir-fry until they turn pink; then remove from wok.

Add another 15 ml (1 tbsp) of peanut oil, and stir-fry the drained wood fungus and the onion for 1 minute; remove from wok.

Heat the remaining 15 ml (1 tbsp) of oil and stir-fry the asparagus on high heat for 1 minute; then turn the heat low, add 60 ml (4 tbsp) of water and cook, covered, for 3 minutes or until the asparagus is tender but still crisp. If the asparagus is mature it may need a little extra liquid and cooking time, but don't let it become limp.

Return the shrimps to the wok, pour in the sauce ingredients and stir until the sauce boils and thickens slightly. Add the wood fungus and onion, toss through quickly, then serve at once with rice or soft fried noodles.

Unless asparagus is very young, peel with vegetable peeler.

Cut onion half into six wedge-shaped sections.

Stir-fry the asparagus in oil for 1 minute.

Steamed Scallops in Shells

Serves 4–6
225 g (8 oz) scallops
1.25 ml (¼ tsp) grated
    fresh ginger
5 ml (1 tsp) oyster sauce
15 ml (1 tbsp) Chinese
    wine or dry sherry
2.5 ml (½ tsp) sugar
1 spring onion
25 g (1 oz) ham

Scallop shells are available very cheaply in some fish-mongers.

Check the number of scallops when buying – there should be at least 12, so that each person can have two or more scallops. Remove the dark vein from the scallops but leave the red roe attached.

Combine the ginger, oyster sauce, wine and sugar; add the scallops and stir to mix. Cover and chill for 30 minutes or longer.

Put one or two scallops on each shell (depending on size of the shells) and place them in a bamboo steamer. Cut the spring onion and ham into fine shreds and sprinkle them over the scallops.

Have a wok of boiling water ready, and place the bamboo steamer on this. Cover the steamer and cook over a moderately high heat for 5 minutes. Serve immediately.

Sprinkle scallops with spring onion and ham.

Steam over boiling water.

Crystal Prawns with Mange-tout

Serves 4
450 g (1 lb) raw prawns
salt
1 egg white
15 ml (1 tbsp) cornflour
15 ml (1 tbsp) oil
100 g (4 oz) mange-tout
1 small clove garlic
pinch of sugar
5 ml (1 tsp) finely grated

fresh ginger
oil for deep frying
Sauce:
125 ml (4 fl oz) chicken
  stock
15 ml (1 tbsp) oyster sauce
15 ml (1 tbsp) Chinese
  wine or dry sherry
5 ml (1 tsp) sesame oil
10 ml (2 tsp) cornflour

Like many Chinese recipes, there are two steps and two methods of cooking combined which makes this an ideal dish for preparing ahead, leaving only the final stir-frying to be done at serving time.

Shell and de-vein the prawns. Slit them more than halfway through from the outer curve. Put the prawns in a large bowl, sprinkle with 5 ml (1 tsp) of salt and stir the prawns briskly for 1 minute.

Transfer prawns to a colander and rinse under cold running water for 1 minute, turning them over and over. Drain, return them to the bowl and sprinkle with another 5 ml (1 tsp) of salt. Repeat the procedure, stirring vigorously for 1 minute, then rinse as before. Drain and repeat a third time. (This removes the slippery feel and strong smell that prawns sometimes have.) Dry the prawns thoroughly on absorbent kitchen paper.

Now marinate the prawns in a 'velveting' mixture which gives them a protective coating and keeps them moist. Sprinkle them with 2.5 ml (½ tsp) salt. Beat the egg white only enough to break it up, and pour it over the prawns. Sprinkle with the cornflour and mix well. Pour the 15 ml (1 tbsp) of oil over and mix. Refrigerate for 1 hour.

String the mange-tout, wash and dry them. Crush the garlic with sugar. Mix all sauce ingredients together.

Place a wok over high heat until it is very hot. Pour in 850 ml (1½ pints) oil and turn the heat to medium. The oil should not be too hot. Drop in the prawns and stir to keep them separate. They will turn white in less than a minute. Lift them immediately from the oil.

Pour off the oil. Wipe out the wok with absorbent kitchen paper and once more place it over high heat. When very hot, add 15 ml (1 tbsp) of oil and swirl to coat the surface. Add the garlic and ginger, and stir for 10 seconds; then add the mange-tout and stir-fry over high heat until they turn a brilliant green (about 1 minute).

Stir the sauce mixture to ensure that the cornflour is smoothly mixed. Pour it into the wok and stir constantly until it boils and thickens. Return the prawns, mix with the sauce and serve immediately with rice.

Sprinkle prawns with salt and stir briskly with chopsticks for 1 minute.

Pour slightly mixed egg white over prawns before adding cornflour.

Fireworks Prawns

Shell the prawns but leave the tails and last segment of shell. Make a shallow slit and remove the dark vein. Split the prawns halfway through the curve of the back and open them out flat, pressing with the palm of your hand. Cut the rind off the bacon and divide the rashers into pieces about the same size as the prawns. Place a piece of bacon on each prawn, pressing together.

Prepare the batter. Beat the eggs until frothy. Sift the flour and salt together, and add all at once to the eggs, beating until the batter is smooth.

Have the onion and other vegetable ingredients for the sauce ready for stir-frying. Mix together the remaining ingredients for the sauce, stirring honey to dissolve.

Heat a wok, add 45 ml (3 tbsp) of peanut oil and swirl to coat the sides of the wok. Add the onion, garlic, ginger and chillies and fry over medium low heat, stirring frequently, until the onion pieces are soft and golden. Add the spring onions and fry for 1 minute. Then add the liquid sauce ingredients, allow to boil, stir and remove the sauce from the wok.

Wash the wok, return it to the heat and add 850 ml (1½ pints) peanut oil for deep frying. When the oil is hot, dip each prawn together with its bacon into the batter, then drop immediately into the hot oil and deep fry until puffed and golden. Fry a few at a time and remove them as soon as they are done – do not overcook. Drain on absorbent kitchen paper.

For convenience, the prawns may be fried and the sauce made an hour or so ahead. Just before serving, reheat the oil until very hot and double-fry the prawns, a few at a time, for just a few seconds. This enhances the crispness. Have sauce ready, reheated in a small pan.

Arrange the prawns on a serving plate and spoon the sauce over. Garnish with spring onion curls.

Press a piece of bacon onto each flattened prawn.

Coat the prawns in batter then deep fry.

Serves 4
450 g (1 lb) large raw prawns
6 rashers streaky bacon
peanut oil for cooking
Batter:
2 eggs
50 g (2 oz) flour
2.5 ml (½ tsp) salt
Sauce:
1 onion, finely chopped
10 ml (2 tsp) finely grated garlic
10 ml (2 tsp) finely grated fresh ginger

3 fresh red chillies, seeded and sliced
8 spring onions, cut into 5 cm (2 inch) lengths
125 ml (4 fl oz) tomato ketchup
30 ml (2 tbsp) Oriental-style sweet chilli sauce
30 ml (2 tbsp) Chinese wine or dry sherry
15 ml (1 tbsp) light soy sauce
15 ml (1 tbsp) honey
1.25 ml (¼ tsp) salt

Lobster in Black Bean Sauce

Serves 4

1 fresh live lobster or
    frozen raw lobster tail
1 large clove garlic,
    unpeeled
2 spring onions
1 egg
3 slices fresh ginger
60 ml (4 tbsp) peanut oil
Sauce:
15–30 ml (1–2 tbsp)
    canned salted black
    beans
2 cloves garlic
5 ml (1 tsp) sugar
5 ml (1 tsp) finely grated
    fresh ginger
175 ml (6 fl oz) hot stock
    or water
30 ml (2 tbsp) Chinese
    wine or dry sherry
15 ml (1 tbsp) light soy
    sauce
10 ml (2 tsp) cornflour

Prepare the lobster (see page 65) – or thaw the frozen lobster tail. Chop straight through where the head joins the body, if using whole lobster. Cut in half lengthways and discard the stomach (in the head) and the feathery tissue. Chop each half of the tail into four or five pieces.

Split the unpeeled garlic clove in two. Cut the spring onions into diagonal slices. Beat the egg slightly, just until mixed.

Prepare the sauce ingredients. Rinse the black beans in a strainer under cold water for a few seconds, drain well, then mash with a fork or chop finely. Crush the 2 cloves of garlic with sugar. Combine the mashed beans, garlic and grated ginger in a small bowl. Mix together the stock (or water), wine and soy sauce. Mix the cornflour smoothly with 15 ml (1 tbsp) of cold water.

Heat a wok, add the peanut oil and when the oil is hot, fry the halved clove of garlic and the slices of ginger until they are brown; then scoop them out and discard. Add the pieces of lobster to the flavoured oil and stir-fry until the shells are bright red (2 to 3 minutes). Remove to a plate.

Pour off the oil, leaving about 15 ml (1 tbsp). Fry the black bean mixture, stirring, until the garlic is fragrant (about 1 minute). Add the liquid ingredients and the pieces of lobster, bring quickly to the boil, then cover the wok and cook on medium heat for 3 minutes.

Uncover pan, stir the cornflour mixture again and pour it into the sauce. Stir until it boils and thickens. Add the spring onions and beaten egg, and stir so that the egg sets in shreds. Serve at once with steamed rice.

If using frozen lobster tail, cut into large pieces.

Finely chop or mash rinsed black beans.

Stir in beaten egg until it sets in shreds.

Deep Fried Lobster with Ginger

There are two ways to treat this recipe. For a delicate result, use only ginger and spring onions. For a more robust flavour, add chillies and garlic. Choose whichever version suits your palate or your mood.

Immobilize the lobster by whichever method you choose (see page 65). Chop straight through where the head joins the body. Cut in half lengthways down both body and head. Discard the stomach (to be found in the head) and the feathery tissue. Chop each half of the tail into four or five pieces. Chop off and discard the pointed tips of the legs. Sprinkle the 15 ml (1 tbsp) of cornflour over the lobster pieces and mix.

Heat a wok, pour in the peanut oil and allow it to get very hot. Discard any fluid that has seeped out of the lobster and drop the pieces into the boiling oil. Scoop the oil over the lobster as it fries. In about 1 to 2 minutes, the shell should turn bright red and the meat loses its transparent look and turns white. The lobster will not be completely cooked at this stage; it finishes cooking with the flavouring ingredients. (If you cook by electricity or your cooker doesn't deliver much heat, it may be better to fry the lobster in two batches, allowing the oil to get very hot again after the first batch has been removed.)

Pour both lobster and oil into a wire sieve set over a heatproof bowl.

Return the wok to the heat with the oil that clings to the sides. Add the ginger, spring onions, chilli and garlic, and stir-fry on high heat for a few seconds. Put in the lobster pieces, pour in the hot chicken stock, cover the wok and cook on high heat for 2–3 minutes so that the lobster finishes cooking in the steam. Uncover and stir. The liquid should be reduced by half.

Blend the cornflour with 15 ml (1 tbsp) of cold water and stir it into the wok; keep stirring until the sauce boils and thickens. Turn off the heat, take 15 ml (1 tbsp) of the oil the lobster was fried in and sprinkle it over the lobster. Toss quickly. This gives a nice gloss. Serve immediately.

Serves 4

1 fresh live lobster, about 900 g (2 lb)
15 ml (1 tbsp) cornflour
1 litre (1¾ pints) peanut oil
15 ml (1 tbsp) fine shreds of fresh ginger
2–3 spring onions, cut into 5 cm (2 inch) lengths
5 ml (1 tsp) sliced hot chilli
5 ml (1 tsp) finely chopped garlic
250 ml (8 fl oz) chicken stock, heated
additional 10 ml (2 tsp) cornflour

Chop the lobster tail into pieces.

Ladle oil over lobster as it fries.

Add blended cornflour and stir until sauce boils and thickens.

Saucy Chilli Crab

Serves 4
2 live crabs
125 ml (4 fl oz) peanut oil
10 ml (2 tsp) finely grated
   fresh ginger
7.5 ml (1½ tsp) finely
   chopped garlic
3 fresh red chillies, seeded
   and chopped
60 ml (4 tbsp) chopped
   fresh coriander for
   garnish
Sauce:
125 ml (4 fl oz) tomato
   ketchup
60 ml (4 tbsp)
   Oriental-style chilli
   sauce
15 ml (1 tbsp) sugar
5 ml (1 tsp) salt

Immobilize the crabs (see page 65). Wash them well, scrubbing away any mossy patches on the shell. Remove the hard top shell or carapace, and reserve these for garnishing. Lift the 'apron' with the tip of a knife and twist off, together with the dark vein. Discard the stomach bag and the feathery grey gills arranged in two rows. Twist off the large claws and chop each claw in half at the joint. Crack the shells with blunt edge of a cleaver so that the sauce can penetrate. Chop the bodies in half down the middle, then cut each half in two again, crossways. Leave legs attached but chop off the pointed tips.

Stir the sauce ingredients together to dissolve the sugar, adding 50 ml (2 fl oz) hot water.

Heat a wok, add the peanut oil and when the oil is hot, fry each carapace until it turns a bright red, just a few seconds. Lift out and reserve. Add the pieces of crab and stir-fry, turning them to cook on all sides until the shells are bright red and the flesh is white and opaque. Remove to a plate.

Turn the heat to low, add the ginger, garlic and chillies and fry until they are cooked but not brown. Add the sauce mixture. Return the crab pieces and spoon the sauce over them until all are coated. Cover the wok and cook on low heat for 2 to 3 minutes. Arrange on a serving dish and garnish with top shell. Sprinkle with chopped coriander leaves, and serve with steamed rice.

To remove top shell, insert knife at back seam and twist.

Crack the claws with cleaver.

Cut each crab half into two, crossways.

Stir-Fried Prawns with Broccoli and Red Ginger

Serves 4

12–16 large raw prawns
1 head firm, fresh broccoli
15 ml (1 tbsp) peanut oil
2.5 ml (½ tsp) finely
grated fresh ginger
15 ml (1 tbsp) fine strips
of red ginger
Sauce:
50 ml (2 fl oz) water
30 ml (2 tbsp) Chinese
wine or dry sherry
15 ml (1 tbsp) light soy
sauce
15 ml (1 tbsp) oyster sauce
2.5 ml (½ tsp) sugar
10 ml (2 tsp) cornflour or
arrowroot
15 ml (1 tbsp) cold water

Shell and de-vein the prawns, leaving the tails on. With the point of a sharp knife make a small slit through the underside of the prawns.

Wash the broccoli and shake dry. Divide into florets, leaving a piece of tender green stalk on each. Pass the end of the stem through the slit in the prawn so that the floret rests within the curve.

Heat the wok and add the oil. When the oil is hot, add the ginger and stir, then immediately add the prawns threaded with broccoli. Stir-fry for two minutes. Add all the sauce ingredients mixed together, except the corn-flour and cold water. Turn the head to medium low, cover and simmer for 3 minutes. Push the prawns to the side of the wok, add the cornflour mixed smoothly with cold water and stir until thick. Serve at once, garnished with red ginger and accompanied by white rice.

Shell and de-vein the prawns, leaving the tails on.

Using a sharp knife, make a small slit through the under-side of the prawns.

Pass a broccoli floret through each prawn.

Chilli Squid

Serves 4

450 g (1 lb) medium-sized
   squid
2.5 ml (½ tsp) salt
1 egg white
30 ml (2 tbsp) cornflour
30 ml (2 tbsp) peanut oil
1 small red pepper
   (capsicum)
6 spring onions
15 ml (1 tbsp) bottled
   preserved hot radish
1 clove garlic
peanut oil for frying
12 mange-tout or tender
   green beans
2 fresh red chillies for
   garnish

Sauce:
125 ml (4 fl oz) light stock
   or water
2.5 ml (½ tsp) each salt
   and sugar
5 ml (1 tsp) chilli oil or
   15 ml (1 tbsp) chilli
   sauce
10 ml (2 tsp) cornflour or
   arrowroot

Hold down the head of the squid with the blunt edge of
a knife and pull the body. The head and contents of sac
will come away. Reserve the tentacles and discard everything else. Slit the body of the squid lengthways and rinse
well.

On the inside surface make diagonal cuts with a sharp
knife held at a 45° angle, parallel to each other and about
6 mm (¼ inch) apart. Then score across these lines to
make a pattern of small diamonds or squares. Take care
not to cut through the squid. After scoring, divide the
squid into neat pieces, about 5 cm × 2.5 cm (2 inch × 1
inch).

In a bowl, mix the squid with salt, egg white, cornflour
and peanut oil. Refrigerate for at least 30 minutes.

Cut the pepper into thin strips and the spring onions
into bite-size lengths. String the mange-tout. Crush the
garlic with a little salt.

Heat a wok over high heat, pour in 450 ml (14 fl oz)
peanut oil and when the oil is moderately hot, drop in the
squid, stirring to separate the pieces. In less than a minute
they will curl and the scoring forms an attractive pattern.
It is important not to overcook or the squid will toughen.
Drain on a wire spoon placed over a heatproof bowl.

Return the wok to the heat with just the oil that clings
to the sides. Stir-fry the garlic, pepper, spring onions and
mange-tout for 1 minute, add the preserved hot radish
and stir. Add the sauce ingredients mixed together and
stir constantly until it boils and thickens. Return the squid
to the pan and mix with the sauce.

Arrange on a serving dish, garnish with chilli flowers
and serve immediately with plain steamed rice.

Note: As an indication of the fiery chilli nature of a dish,
I like to garnish it with chilli flowers but remember to slit
and soak chillies in ice water some hours before required,
as they take time to curl.

*Hold the squid head and
pull the body with the other
hand. The head and
contents of the sac will come
away.*

*Score the body of the squid
in a diamond pattern.*

*The squid will curl when
cooked in hot oil. Do not
overcook.*

*Stir-fry garlic, pepper,
spring onions, mange-tout.*

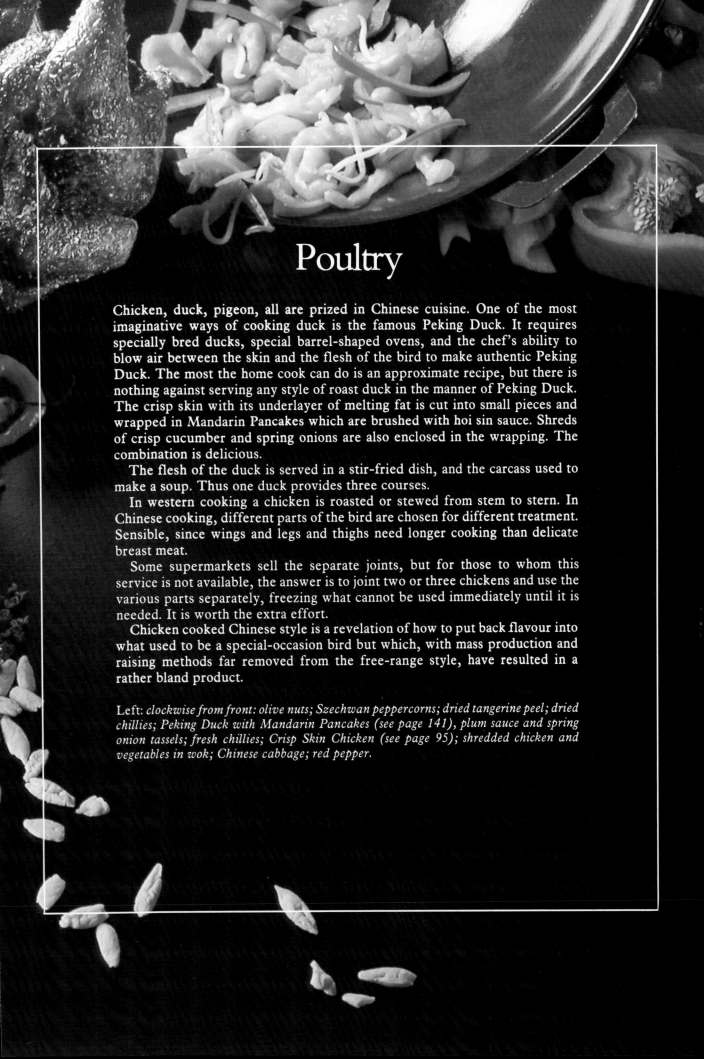

Poultry

Chicken, duck, pigeon, all are prized in Chinese cuisine. One of the most imaginative ways of cooking duck is the famous Peking Duck. It requires specially bred ducks, special barrel-shaped ovens, and the chef's ability to blow air between the skin and the flesh of the bird to make authentic Peking Duck. The most the home cook can do is an approximate recipe, but there is nothing against serving any style of roast duck in the manner of Peking Duck. The crisp skin with its underlayer of melting fat is cut into small pieces and wrapped in Mandarin Pancakes which are brushed with hoi sin sauce. Shreds of crisp cucumber and spring onions are also enclosed in the wrapping. The combination is delicious.

The flesh of the duck is served in a stir-fried dish, and the carcass used to make a soup. Thus one duck provides three courses.

In western cooking a chicken is roasted or stewed from stem to stern. In Chinese cooking, different parts of the bird are chosen for different treatment. Sensible, since wings and legs and thighs need longer cooking than delicate breast meat.

Some supermarkets sell the separate joints, but for those to whom this service is not available, the answer is to joint two or three chickens and use the various parts separately, freezing what cannot be used immediately until it is needed. It is worth the extra effort.

Chicken cooked Chinese style is a revelation of how to put back flavour into what used to be a special-occasion bird but which, with mass production and raising methods far removed from the free-range style, have resulted in a rather bland product.

Left: clockwise from front: olive nuts; Szechwan peppercorns; dried tangerine peel; dried chillies; Peking Duck with Mandarin Pancakes (see page 141), plum sauce and spring onion tassels; fresh chillies; Crisp Skin Chicken (see page 95); shredded chicken and vegetables in wok; Chinese cabbage; red pepper.

Chicken Livers with Bamboo Shoot and Cabbage

Serves 4

450 g (1 lb) chicken livers
2 slices fresh ginger
1 spring onion
60 ml (4 tbsp) dark soy
sauce
1 canned winter bamboo
shoot
1 bunch Chinese mustard
cabbage (gai choy)
15 ml (1 tbsp) sugar
15 ml (1 tbsp) Chinese
wine or dry sherry
30 ml (2 tbsp) peanut oil
5 ml (1 tsp) cornflour
10 ml (2 tsp) sesame oil
15 ml (1 tbsp) white cider
vinegar

Halve the chicken livers and remove any tubes, connective tissue and yellow spots. Put the livers into a small saucepan with the ginger, spring onion cut into three or four pieces, and 30 ml (2 tbsp) of the soy sauce. Add enough boiling water to just cover the livers. Simmer, covered, over a low heat for 5 minutes. Drain and discard ginger and onion.

Slice the bamboo shoot. Wash the mustard cabbage and slice diagonally; there should be about 350 g (12 oz). Combine the remaining 30 ml (2 tbsp) of soy sauce, sugar and wine.

Heat a wok, add the peanut oil and swirl it around the sides of the wok. Toss in the chicken livers and stir-fry for 10 seconds. Add the soy mixture, bamboo shoot and mustard cabbage, and stir-fry for 2 minutes. Blend the cornflour with 10 ml (2 tsp) of cold water and add this to the livers, stirring until the sauce thickens. Add sesame oil.

Sprinkle the vinegar around the edge of the wok and, as it sizzles into a steam, give the livers a few fast turns. Turn out into a dish to serve.

Halve the chicken livers.

Cut mustard cabbage into slices.

Chicken Velvet Fu Yung

Serves 4
1 large chicken breast,
    about 350 g (12 oz)
5 ml (1 tsp) salt
10 ml (2 tsp) water
    chestnut flour or
    cornflour
15 ml (1 tbsp) Chinese
    wine or dry sherry
4 eggs, separated
1 stem celery
1 Chinese cabbage or
    lettuce
peanut oil for cooking
5 ml (1 tsp) sugar
2.5 ml (½ tsp) salt
Sauce:
stock made with chicken
    skin and bones
5 ml (1 tsp) light soy sauce
15 ml (1 tbsp) cornflour

Scrape chicken flesh finely.

Stir whipped egg whites into chicken mixture.

Chop cooked egg yolk with wok chan.

'Chicken velvet' is a term that describes very finely puréed chicken meat which has been lightened by the addition of water and egg whites. When cooked, it is similar to a soft custard. ('Velveting', on the other hand, is a method of marinating and coating.) Fu Yung is a white hibiscus and this dish is so named because the chicken should remain white when cooked.

Remove the skin and bones from the chicken breast. When boning, hold a sharp knife close to the bone.

Take the small fillet from each side of the breast and, holding the silvery tendon, scrape the flesh finely. Discard tendon.

Place the large fillets on the chopping board, with the side that was next to the skin downwards. Again use the sharp chopper to scrape the flesh free of the long fibres that lie against the skin.

Put the skin, bones and discarded fibres into a small pan with about 350 ml (12 fl oz) cold water to cover, and simmer to give the 250 ml (8 fl oz) chicken stock needed for the sauce. Strain and season to taste with salt.

Finely chop the chicken meat, first one way and then the other, until it is a fine purée. Gradually add 15 ml (1 tbsp) of cold water while chopping, to lighten the consistency. Add the salt and wine. Add the water chestnut flour or cornflour mixed smoothly with 15 ml (1 tbsp) of cold water, stirring to mix.

In a large bowl whip the whites of the eggs until frothy and holding soft peaks. Stir a large spoonful at a time into the chicken mixture until all the egg white is incorporated. Cover and chill for 30 minutes or longer.

Beat the yolks with a little salt and set aside. Cut the celery into thin slices. Cut the cabbage or lettuce into chunky pieces.

Heat a wok, add 15 ml (1 tbsp) of peanut oil and stir the egg yolk over medium heat until it sets. Do not brown. Remove from heat, cut into small pieces with the sharp edge of a wok chan.

Heat another 15 ml (1 tbsp) of peanut oil and stir-fry the celery for 1 minute, not allowing it to brown; set aside.

Heat another 30 ml (2 tbsp) of peanut oil and stir-fry the cabbage or lettuce for 1 minute. Sprinkle with the sugar and salt. Add 30 ml (2 tbsp) of water, cover the wok and leave for 30 seconds for lettuce or 2 to 3 minutes for a firmer green vegetable. Spread on the serving dish.

Clean out the wok, return it to the heat and when hot, pour in 125 ml (4 fl oz) peanut oil. Do not let the oil become too hot – the aim is to keep the chicken from browning. Pour in the chicken velvet and turn it quickly with the wok chan until it is white. Pour it through a wire strainer and let all excess oil drain out.

Meanwhile combine the sauce ingredients including 250 ml (8 fl oz) of chicken stock, and bring to a boil in a small saucepan, stirring until thick and clear. Toss the chicken velvet with celery and yolk pieces, spread over the green vegetable, and pour the sauce over. Serve at once with rice.

Braised Ginger Chicken

Cut the chicken into bite-size pieces. Scrape the skin off the ginger and cut the ginger into thin slices, then into fine shreds. Set aside. Crush the garlic with a sprinkling of salt.

Heat the peppercorns lightly in a dry pan. Then crush them with a pestle and mortar or on a wooden chopping board using the handle of a heavy chopper.

Heat a wok over high heat, add the peanut oil and fry the shredded ginger and crushed garlic over low heat until pale golden. Add the chicken pieces, raise the heat to medium and fry until the chicken changes colour. Add pepper, wine, honey, soy sauce and star anise. Cover the wok and simmer over low heat for 25 minutes or until the chicken is tender, adding a little hot water toward end of cooking if necessary. Serve with hot steamed rice.

Serves 6

1.4 kg (3 lb) roasting chicken
1 piece fresh tender ginger
1 clove garlic
2.5 ml (½ tsp) Szechwan peppercorns or black peppercorns
60 ml (4 tbsp) peanut oil
50 ml (2 fl oz) Chinese wine or dry sherry
15 ml (1 tbsp) honey
50 ml (2 fl oz) light soy sauce
1 star anise

Cut ginger into fine shreds.

Fry chicken until it changes colour.

Chicken with Peppery Turnips

Finely chop the peppery turnips.

Separate the soaked noodles so they cook evenly.

Serves 4
450 g (1 lb) chicken breast or thighs
2.5 ml (½ tsp) salt
20 ml (4 tsp) egg white
10 ml (2 tsp) cornflour
peanut oil for mixing and cooking – about 125 ml (4 fl oz)
12 green beans
1 small carrot
30 ml (2 tbsp) sesame seeds
10 ml (2 tsp) finely grated fresh ginger
30 ml (2 tbsp) peppery turnips
3 small bundles fine egg noodles, about 175 g (6 oz)
2 spring onions, coarsely chopped
Sauce:
stock made with chicken skin and bones
15 ml (1 tbsp) light soy sauce
15 ml (1 tbsp) Chinese wine or dry sherry
10 ml (2 tsp) oyster sauce
10 ml (2 tsp) cornflour

If you like your dishes with a dash of fire, introduce peppery turnips or preserved hot radish or preserved Szechwan vegetable. They come in jars or cans and all add an interesting flavour.

Skin and bone the chicken pieces and cut the chicken meat into small dice. Place in a bowl and mix in the salt and egg white. Then add the cornflour and mix again. Add 10 ml (2 tsp) of peanut oil and mix. Cover the bowl and chill for at least 30 minutes.

Make a small quantity of stock from the chicken skin and bones and about 250 ml (8 fl oz) water.

Top and tail the beans and string them if necessary; cut them into small slices. Dice the carrot to make pieces of similar size. Cook the beans and the carrots separately in a little boiling water for 1 or 2 minutes, just until half-tender. Drain, and place them in ice-cold water to set their colour.

Toast the sesame seeds in a dry pan over low heat until golden. Remove from the pan and set aside.

Soak the grated ginger in 15 ml (1 tbsp) of cold water, then squeeze out the juice through a small strainer. Finely chop the peppery turnips.

Soak the noodles in hot water to loosen and separate the strands. Bring a saucepan of water to the boil with a little salt and 5 ml (1 tsp) of peanut oil. Drain the noodles and drop them into the boiling water, boil for 2 minutes or until just cooked, not mushy. Run cold water over to cool, drain well.

Heat a wok, add 45 ml (3 tbsp) of peanut oil and swirl to coat the sides of the wok. When the oil is hot, add the noodles, tossing and stirring to heat them through. Place on a serving dish, cover with foil and keep warm.

Mix the sauce ingredients together, including 125 ml cup (4 fl oz) chicken stock.

Heat the wok again, add 60 ml (4 tbsp) of peanut oil. When the oil is moderately hot, add the chicken meat and stir for 1 minute or just until it has turned white. Add the green beans, carrots, ginger juice and turnips and stir-fry for 30 seconds. Add the sauce mixture and the spring onions, stirring while the sauce boils and thickens. Ladle it over the noodles. Sprinkle with the toasted sesame seeds and serve at once.

Home-Style Steamed Chicken

Serves 4 as part of a Chinese meal, serves 2 as a single dish with rice
half a 1.4 kg (3 lb) roasting chicken
10 ml (2 tsp) light soy sauce
10 ml (2 tsp) Chinese wine or dry sherry
10 ml (2 tsp) cornflour
5 ml (1 tsp) finely chopped fresh ginger
2.5 ml (½ tsp) salt
2.5 ml (½ tsp) sugar
2.5 ml (½ tsp) sesame oil, optional

A quick and easy dish with hardly any preparation – delicately flavoured and popular with children as well as grown-ups.

Place the half-chicken on a wooden chopping board and separate the thigh and drumstick from the body. Detach the wing, too. With a sharp, heavy cleaver, chop straight through the bones, cutting the chicken into bite-size pieces. Wipe all cut surfaces with damp absorbent kitchen paper to remove any bits of bone.

Put the chicken on a plate, add all the other ingredients and mix well.

Place the plate in a bamboo or other steamer, or on a trivet or upturned bowl in a large pan containing boiling water. Cover the pan with a lid and steam on high heat for 15 minutes.

If liked, place some Chinese vegetables or chunks of peeled pumpkin on the plate with the chicken. Serve hot with steamed rice.

Chop chicken into small pieces.

Steam the chicken over boiling water.

Red Cooked Chicken and Mushrooms

Serves 4–6

8–10 large dried Chinese
mushrooms
1.4 kg (3 lb) chicken
350 ml (12 fl oz) dark soy
sauce
75 ml (3 fl oz) Chinese
wine or dry sherry
sesame oil
5 cm (2 inch) piece fresh
ginger, peeled and
sliced
1 clove garlic, peeled
1 whole star anise
30 ml (2 tbsp) sugar
15 ml (1 tbsp) peanut oil
Chinese cabbage

*Baste chicken frequently
with the cooking liquid.*

*Cut cooked chicken into
bite-size pieces.*

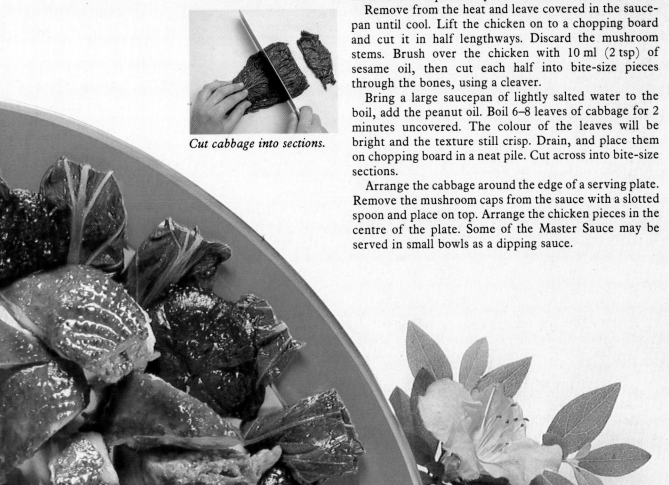

Cut cabbage into sections.

Red cooking is done in quite a large amount of soy sauce, but it must be dark soy or the dish would not have its rich colour and the proper flavour. Light soy sauce is more salty, too. While it may seem like an extravagant use of soy sauce, the cooking liquid that remains is a Master Sauce. It can be frozen and used over and over again to simmer meats and poultry.

Soak the mushrooms in 350 ml (12 fl oz) boiling water for 30 minutes. Drain and reserve the liquid.

Wash the chicken under cold running water and drain well. Cut off the mushroom stems and put them into the cavity of the chicken for flavouring. These will be discarded after cooking.

Choose a saucepan into which the chicken will just fit so that the liquid will cover as much of the bird as possible. Put the chicken into the saucepan breast down, then add the liquid from the mushrooms, the soy sauce, wine, 10 ml (2 tsp) of sesame oil, ginger, garlic, star anise, sugar and the mushroom caps. Bring slowly to the boil, then turn the heat low, cover the saucepan and simmer very gently for 15 minutes.

Using tongs, turn the chicken over, replace the lid and simmer for 20 minutes more. Baste the breast of the chicken with liquid every 5 minutes.

Remove from the heat and leave covered in the saucepan until cool. Lift the chicken on to a chopping board and cut it in half lengthways. Discard the mushroom stems. Brush over the chicken with 10 ml (2 tsp) of sesame oil, then cut each half into bite-size pieces through the bones, using a cleaver.

Bring a large saucepan of lightly salted water to the boil, add the peanut oil. Boil 6–8 leaves of cabbage for 2 minutes uncovered. The colour of the leaves will be bright and the texture still crisp. Drain, and place them on chopping board in a neat pile. Cut across into bite-size sections.

Arrange the cabbage around the edge of a serving plate. Remove the mushroom caps from the sauce with a slotted spoon and place on top. Arrange the chicken pieces in the centre of the plate. Some of the Master Sauce may be served in small bowls as a dipping sauce.

Braised Chicken with Five Flavours

Serves 6
1.1 kg (2½ lb) chicken
1 mandarin or orange
5 ml (1 tsp) Szechwan
   peppercorns
45 ml (3 tbsp) oil
15 ml (1 tbsp) finely
   chopped fresh ginger
3 dried red chillies
3 fresh red chillies
3 spring onions, finely
   sliced
5 ml (1 tsp) salt
Sauce:
30 ml (2 tbsp) Chinese
   wine or dry sherry
30 ml (2 tbsp) dark soy
   sauce
5 ml (1 tsp) sugar
juice from the mandarin
   or orange
10 ml (2 tsp) sesame oil

Not all Chinese food must be made and served at once. Here is a good do-ahead dish.

Cut the chicken in half lengthways, then chop through the bones into pieces about 2.5 cm (1 inch) wide.

Squeeze 45 ml (3 tbsp) of juice from the mandarin and set this aside for the sauce. Finely shred the orange portion of the rind, first removing all the white pith.

Roast the peppercorns in a dry pan until fragrant. Pound them with a pestle and mortar or with the handle of a cleaver.

Heat a wok, add the peanut oil and swirl to coat the sides of the wok. When the oil is hot, put in the ginger, dried and fresh chillies, shredded rind and half of the spring onions. Toss for about 10 seconds. Add half the chicken pieces, brown over high heat and remove from the wok.

Brown the remaining chicken pieces, then return the first batch of chicken to the wok and sprinkle with salt and the Szechwan pepper. Mix together the ingredients for the sauce, except sesame oil, and pour in. Cover the wok and simmer for 25 to 30 minutes, turning the pieces of chicken every 10 minutes so that they will be evenly coloured. Add remaining spring onions.

Uncover and, if sauce is thin, cook on high heat for a few minutes, stirring, until it becomes thick and syrupy. Turn off the heat, remove and discard the chillies, add sesame oil and mix well. Serve with hot steamed rice.

If not serving the dish straight away, remove from the wok and reheat before serving.

Finely shred the mandarin rind.

Pound roasted peppercorns with the handle of a cleaver.

Sprinkle salt and ground peppercorns over chicken.

Lemon Chicken with Olive Nuts or Pine Nuts

Bone the chicken and remove the skin. Cut the chicken into finger-width strips. Place the pieces in a bowl, add the salt, ginger and egg yolks; mix well. Sprinkle the cornflour over and mix again. Cover the bowl and chill for at least 30 minutes.

Combine sauce ingredients in a small bowl, with 180 ml (12 tbsp) of water.

Heat a wok, add about 450 ml (¾ pint) peanut oil and when hot, drop in the chicken, one piece at a time until one-third of the pieces have been added. Fry over medium heat until the chicken meat is cooked through but do not allow to brown – cut a piece of chicken in half to test. Drain the cooked pieces, then cook remaining chicken meat in the same way.

When chicken has been removed from the wok, turn the heat very low and fry the olive nuts to a pale golden colour. Lift out on to absorbent kitchen paper. Drain the oil into a heatproof container.

Return the wok to the heat, pour in the sauce mixture, first giving it a little stir to ensure that the cornflour has not settled at the bottom. Stir until it boils and thickens. Add the lemon slices and sesame oil. Return the chicken meat and olive nuts, toss quickly to coat, and serve immediately. Garnish with fresh coriander and extra lemon slices.

Serves 4–6
700 g (1½ lb) chicken thighs or 450 g (1 lb) chicken breasts
5 ml (1 tsp) salt
2.5 ml (½ tsp) grated fresh ginger
2 egg yolks
20 ml (4 tsp) cornflour
peanut oil for deep frying
25 g (1 oz) Chinese olive nuts or pine nuts
6 lemon slices
5 ml (1 tsp) sesame oil
Lemon Sauce:
20 ml (4 tsp) lemon juice
30 ml (2 tbsp) sugar
10 ml (2 tsp) light soy sauce
2 drops yellow food colouring
20 ml (4 tsp) cornflour
Garnish:
sprigs of fresh coriander
additional lemon slices

Cut the chicken into finger-width strips.

Deep fry the chicken pieces until cooked but not brown.

Chinese olive nuts.

Chicken with Pecans

Remove bones from chicken breasts.

Cut each straw mushroom in half.

Remove strings from mange-tout.

Serves 4–5
450 g (1 lb) chicken breast
2.5 ml (½ tsp) salt
15 ml (1 tbsp) Chinese
  wine or dry sherry
1 egg white
15 ml (1 tbsp) cornflour
450 ml (¾ pint) peanut oil
50 g (2 oz) drained canned
  straw mushrooms
100 g (4 oz) mange-tout
75 g (3 oz) pecan halves
5 ml (1 tsp) crushed garlic
5 ml (1 tsp) grated fresh
  ginger
Sauce:
stock made with chicken
  skin and bones
15 ml (1 tbsp) oyster sauce
15 ml (1 tbsp) Chinese
  wine or dry sherry
5 ml (1 tsp) cornflour

Remove the skin and bones from the chicken and cut the chicken meat into small dice. Place in a bowl and season with the salt and wine. Beat the egg white slightly and add to chicken, mixing well. Leave for 10 minutes.

Mix the cornflour into the chicken. Add 15 ml (1 tbsp) of the peanut oil and mix, then refrigerate for at least 30 minutes.

Make a small quantity of stock from the chicken skin and bones and about 250 ml (8 fl oz) water.

Drain the straw mushrooms well and cut each in half. Remove the strings from the mange-tout.

Heat the remaining peanut oil in a wok and fry the pecans over a medium heat, taking care not to burn them. Remove when golden, and drain.

In the same oil over medium heat, deep fry the chicken, stirring to separate pieces, just until the meat turns white. Drain.

Pour off all but 15 ml (1 tbsp) of oil. Fry the garlic and ginger in this remaining oil until golden. Add the straw mushrooms and stir-fry for 2 minutes. Add the mange-tout and stir-fry for 1 minute.

Combine the ingredients for the sauce including 125 ml (4 fl oz) chicken stock; add this to the wok and stir until the sauce boils and thickens.

Return the chicken to the wok and stir with other ingredients just until heated through. Turn off the heat, toss in the pecans, mix through and serve immediately.

Note: For a more pungent flavour, toss the fried pecans while hot in a mixture of 2.5 ml (½ tsp) garlic salt and 2.5 ml (½ tsp) chilli powder.

Deep Fried Crisp-Skin Chicken

Serves 4–6
900 kg (2 lb) chicken
5 ml (1 tsp) salt
12.5 ml (2½ tsp) five spice
  powder
10 ml (2 tsp) ground
  cinnamon
5 ml (1 tsp) cayenne
  pepper
30 ml (2 tbsp) honey
1 lemon, sliced
peanut oil for deep frying
Salt and Spice Mix:
30 ml (2 tbsp) salt
5 ml (1 tsp) Szechwan
  peppercorns
2.5 ml (½ tsp) five spice
  powder
Garnish:
sprigs of fresh coriander
lemon wedges

Pour hot honey mixture over chicken.

Lower chicken into wok and ladle oil over.

Chop chicken into strips to serve.

Wash the chicken and wipe it with absorbent kitchen paper inside and out. Mix the salt with 2.5 ml (½ tsp) of the five spice powder and rub this inside the chicken. Place it in a large heatproof bowl.

Bring to the boil 1.5 litres (2½ pints) water with the cinnamon, cayenne pepper and the remaining 10 ml (2 tsp) of five spice powder; and pour it over the chicken. Leave the chicken in this while bringing to the boil 1 litre (1¾ pints) water with the honey and lemon slices.

Drain the chicken from the spice mixture and put it in a colander. Slowly pour the honey mixture over, making sure it comes into contact with all parts of the chicken. Put it on a wire rack in an airy place to dry – in front of a window or in the sunlight would be ideal. Leave it to dry for 5 hours.

Tie the legs of the chicken together, leaving sufficient string to hold it with while frying. Shortly before serving, heat about 2 litres (3½ pints) of peanut oil in a wok and lower the bird into the oil. With a ladle, spoon oil over the chicken as it cooks, and turn it so that it is cooked and brown on all sides. On medium heat the chicken should be cooked through in about 12 to 15 minutes. Test by piercing with a fine skewer where the thigh joins the body. If the juice runs out clear, the chicken is done; but if it is pink, return the chicken to the pan for further cooking.

Lift on to a board with a slotted spoon and cut the chicken in half lengthways with a heavy chopper. Place each half with cut side downwards on the board and chop through into strips 2.5 cm (1 inch) wide. Reassemble the bird on a serving dish. Garnish with fresh coriander sprigs and serve immediately.

Serve with Salt and Spice Mix (see below) and wedges of lemon. The pieces of chicken are sprinkled with a pinch of the salt mix and a few drops of lemon juice by each diner before eating.

Salt and Spice Mix: Put the peppercorns and salt into a small heavy pan over very low heat and roast, shaking the pan, until very hot and the salt starts to colour slightly. Remove the pan from the heat and allow the mixture to cool. When cold, grind with a pestle and mortar or put into a plastic bag and crush with a rolling pin. Mix in the five spice powder. Store in a jar with well-fitting lid.

Chicken with Bean Sprouts and Mixed Pickles

Bone the chicken thighs and discard the skin – or buy chicken thigh fillets. Freeze the meat until firm.

Slice the chicken meat thinly, place it in a bowl and mix in the ginger, wine, salt and cornflour.

Cut the pepper into shreds. Remove the tails from the bean sprouts.

Combine all the sauce ingredients in a small bowl, with 30 ml (2 tbsp) of water.

Heat a wok, add the peanut oil and when hot, fry the chicken mixture, stirring constantly for about 1 minute. Add the pepper and the pickles. Stir in the bean sprouts. Add the sauce mixture and stir over high heat for 1 minute or until the liquid thickens and becomes clear. Serve immediately.

Serves 4
450 g (1 lb) chicken thighs
5 ml (1 tsp) grated fresh ginger
15 ml (1 tbsp) Chinese wine or dry sherry
2.5 ml (½ tsp) salt
10 ml (2 tsp) cornflour
1 small red pepper
225 g (8 oz) bean sprouts

30 ml (2 tbsp) peanut oil
60 ml (4 tbsp) sliced Chinese mixed pickles
Sauce:
30 ml (2 tbsp) Chinese wine or dry sherry
15 ml (1 tbsp) light soy sauce
2.5 ml (½ tsp) sugar
10 ml (2 tsp) cornflour

Chinese mixed pickles.

Slice chicken meat thinly.

Remove tails from bean sprouts.

Hunan-Style Chicken

Serves 4–6

900 g (2 lb) chicken thighs, boned
5 ml (1 tsp) Szechwan peppercorns
2.5 ml (½ tsp) salt
30 ml (2 tbsp) dark soy sauce
30 ml (2 tbsp) Chinese wine or dry sherry
10 ml (2 tsp) sugar
30 ml (2 tbsp) peanut oil
1 or 2 dried red chillies

30 ml (2 tbsp) finely chopped spring onions
10 ml (2 tsp) finely chopped fresh ginger
5 ml (1 tsp) finely chopped garlic
5 ml (1 tsp) sesame oil
30 ml (2 tbsp) Chinese black vinegar or 15 ml (1 tbsp) wine vinegar
5 ml (1 tsp) chilli bean sauce

Flatten boned chicken with cleaver.

Marinate chicken pieces in soy mixture for 30 minutes.

Like the food of its better-known neighbour, Szechwan province, the food of this western area is hot and spicy to contend with the hot and humid climate. This dish is not too pungent and well worth trying.

For this recipe, the dark meat is best and it is possible to buy filleted thighs in some poultry shops. If these are not available, buy thighs and drumsticks, allowing about 225 g (8 oz) extra for the bones. Leave the skin on but remove all the bones, keeping the knife close to the bone so that little meat is wasted.

Lay the boned pieces on a wooden chopping board, skin side down, and flatten them slightly by pounding with the blunt edge of a cleaver or with a meat mallet. Cut into bite-size pieces.

Roast the peppercorns in a dry pan for a few minutes, shaking the pan, until fragrant. Allow to cool, then grind them with a pestle and mortar. Mix with the salt, and sprinkle this over the chicken pieces. Mix and leave for 5 minutes.

Combine the soy sauce, wine and sugar, stir to dissolve the sugar, and pour over the chicken. Turn the chicken pieces well in the marinade. Leave for 30 minutes.

Heat a wok, add the peanut oil and swirl to coat the sides of the wok. Fry the dried chillies for 1 minute. Add the spring onions, ginger and garlic and stir-fry for 10 seconds. Add the chicken together with the marinade and on high heat, stir-fry for a few minutes, just until all the chicken has come into contact with the hot pan. Turn the heat to low, cover the wok and simmer for about 5 minutes or until the chicken is tender.

Meanwhile, mix together the sesame oil, vinegar and chilli bean sauce.

Uncover the wok and if liquid is not thick, raise the heat and turn the chicken pieces over and over using a wok chan (wok spatula). The sauce will become thick and coat the chicken.

Add the sesame oil combination and mix quickly but thoroughly. Transfer to a serving dish immediately and, if liked, discard the dry chillies. Serve with rice and a dish of vegetables.

Duck with Tangerine Sauce

Serves 4–6
1.75 kg (3¾ lb) duck
2.5 ml (½ tsp) salt
2.5 ml (½ tsp) pepper
5 ml (1 tsp) grated fresh ginger
30 ml (2 tbsp) cornflour
oil for deep frying
Sauce:
30 ml (2 tbsp) light soy sauce
15 ml (1 tbsp) sugar
60 ml (4 tbsp) Chinese wine or dry sherry
juice of 3 mandarins or 2 oranges
1 piece dried tangerine peel
Garnish:
segments of mandarin or orange

With a sharp cleaver, chop the duck into 12–14 pieces. Discard the tail. (Neck and wing tips may be added to the stock pot.) Rub the pieces of duck with salt, pepper and ginger, and leave for 2 hours.

Blend 5 ml (1 tsp) of the cornflour with 15 ml (1 tbsp) water and set aside. Toss the duck pieces in the remaining cornflour.

Deep-fry four pieces at a time for 3 to 4 minutes. Drain on absorbent kitchen paper.

In a saucepan, combine the sauce ingredients with 250 ml (8 fl oz) water, bring to the boil and simmer for 2 minutes. Add the duck pieces, cover the saucepan and simmer for 30 to 40 minutes or until the duck is tender. Remove the tangerine peel. Stir the reserved cornflour and water, and mix it into the sauce until it boils and thickens. Serve garnished with mandarin or orange segments gently heated in the sauce if liked.

Chop the duck into 12–14 pieces.

Deep fry floured duck pieces.

Duck with Sweet Hot Plum Sauce

Wash the duck well. Cut off and discard the tail. Dry inside and out with absorbent kitchen paper. Combine salt, soy sauce, wine and five spice powder, and rub all over the duck, inside and out. Leave to marinate for at least 1 hour so the flavours can penetrate.

Put the duck on a steamer rack and steam for 1½ to 2 hours or until tender.

Set the duck aside to cool and when cool enough to handle, dry it thoroughly with absorbent kitchen paper. Dredge the duck with cornflour.

Heat oil in a wok and when very hot, gently lower the duck into the oil. Keep ladling hot oil over the top of the duck. Turn it when the underside is done, and fry the other side in the same manner until the skin is crisp. Lift it out of the oil with a slotted spoon, allowing the oil to drain back into the wok.

Chop the duck in half lengthways, then chop each half into bite-size pieces. Arrange on a serving platter and spoon the sauce over.

Sauce: Heat the 15 ml (1 tbsp) of oil and gently fry the ginger and garlic until fragrant (about 1 minute). Stir in the plum sauce and chilli sauce plus 15 ml (1 tbsp) of water, until the sauce boils. Simmer for 1 minute. Serve with rice and garnish, if liked, with carrot flowers.

Serves 4–5
1.8 kg (4 lb) duck
7.5 ml (1½ tsp) salt
15 ml (1 tbsp) light soy
  sauce
10 ml (2 tsp) Chinese wine
  or dry sherry
5 ml (1 tsp) five spice
  powder
30 ml (2 tbsp) cornflour
oil for deep frying
spring onions or fresh
  coriander for garnish
Sauce:
15 ml (1 tbsp) oil
5 ml (1 tsp) finely grated
  fresh ginger
2.5 ml (½ tsp) crushed
  garlic
60 ml (4 tbsp) bottled
  plum sauce
5 ml (1 tsp) bottled
  Chinese chilli sauce

Rub duck inside and out with spice mixture.

Ladle hot oil over duck until skin is crisp.

Braised Duck with Sweet Potatoes

Red bean curd.

Add the bean curd mixture to the browned duck, then pour in water.

Cut the duck into pieces, Chinese style.

Serves 6
1.8 kg (4 lb) duck
2 cloves garlic, crushed
5 ml (1 tsp) finely grated fresh ginger
15 ml (1 tbsp) light soy sauce
15 ml (1 tbsp) Chinese wine or dry sherry
700 g (1½ lb) sweet potatoes
125 ml (4 fl oz) peanut oil
60 ml (4 tbsp) red bean curd
10 ml (2 tsp) sugar

If the duck has been frozen, allow it to thaw completely. Rinse the duck and wipe inside and out with absorbent kitchen paper. Combine the garlic, ginger, soy sauce and wine, and rub all over the duck, inside and out.

Peel the sweet potatoes, cut them into 5 cm (2 inch) slices and drop into a bowl of cold water.

Heat the oil in a wok and brown the duck all over, turning it frequently. Remove duck to a dish.

Pour off most of the oil, leaving only a little. Return the duck to the wok. Add the bean curd mashed with the sugar. Pour in hot water to come halfway up the duck. Bring to the boil, then reduce the heat, cover the wok and simmer for 1 hour. Turn the duck during cooking, and add more boiling water if necessary.

Drain the sweet potatoes, add them to the wok, and simmer for a further 15 to 30 minutes or until the duck is tender.

Lift the duck on to a wooden board and cut it into pieces with a sharp cleaver, Chinese style. Arrange the duck pieces on a warmed serving dish, spoon the sweet potatoes and gravy over.

Crisp-Fried Boneless Duck

Serves 6–8 as part of a meal
1 duckling, about 1.4 kg
   (3 lb)
350 ml (12 fl oz) dark soy
   sauce
125 ml (4 fl oz) Chinese
   wine or dry sherry
2 whole star anise
2 cloves
2 sticks cinnamon
5 ml (1 tsp) fennel seeds
5 ml (1 tsp) Szechwan
   peppercorns
5 slices fresh ginger
30 ml (2 tbsp) sugar
oil for deep frying
Batter:
100 g (4 oz) self-raising
   flour
pinch of salt
For serving:
plum sauce

Place fried duck in pan with soy mixture.

Remove all bones from the duck.

Dip pieces of duck into batter before frying.

Wash and dry the duck well. Rub it all over with some of the dark soy sauce and set it aside for at least 30 minutes.

In a large saucepan combine the rest of the dark soy sauce with 350 ml (12 fl oz) water, the wine and the spices which have been knotted in a square of muslin. Add ginger and sugar and bring to a gentle simmer.

Heat at least 1.1 litres (2 pints) of oil in a wok for deep frying the duck and when the oil is hot, slide the duck into it. Fry first one side and then the other until it is evenly brown all over.

Lift the duck out of the wok and put it into the saucepan containing the soy mixture. Bring to a simmer, turn the heat very low, cover the saucepan and cook for 1 hour or until the duck is tender when tested. Lift duck out of the sauce and drain in a colander. Allow duck to become cold enough to handle.

Meanwhile, make a thick batter with the self-raising flour, whisking until smooth with sufficient cold water to give a thick coating consistency. Let the batter stand for at least 1 hour.

Lay the duck on its back on a wooden board and, with a sharp chopper, cut through the skin of the duck, right down the middle. Find the breast bone, right below the neck, and wiggle it out. Spread the skin away from the bones as though unzipping a coat down the front. It is now quite easy to lift out the bony framework (use it for making stock).

Turn the duck over, breast downwards, and make slits in the legs and wings. Loosen the bones and coax them out, twisting them free at the joints. Turn duck over again, feel for the thigh bones and remove these as well.

Cut duck in half lengthways and chop the now-boneless duck crossways into strips 2.5 cm (1 inch) wide.

Reheat the oil for the second frying, but do not have it too hot. Dip the pieces of duck into the batter and then slide them into the oil, a few at a time. Spoon the oil over while cooking. When golden brown, lift them out and drain. When all the pieces are fried, place them on a serving platter and spoon plum sauce over. Finish with a bright garnish and serve with hot steamed rice or Mandarin Pancakes (see page 141).

Note: The liquid in which the duck simmered is now a Master Sauce and may be used for cooking other poultry, meat or seafood. Use a spoonful to give good flavour to sauces. It also freezes well.

Meat

In Chinese cuisine, meat is cut into thin slices or shreds so that it cooks quickly. Each piece is small enough not to require further cutting and knives are never used at the table. In the few dishes where meat is cooked in a large piece, it is sliced or diced after cooking and before serving, generally combined with other ingredients. No great piece of meat (as in the western roast) ever appears at the table.

Meat is synonymous with pork in China. Pigs are easy to raise, live on scraps and are within the means of most people.

Lamb is not favoured except in the northern provinces, since to the Chinese palate its flavour is too strong. In those dishes where it is used, there is no denying the skill of the chefs in giving it more pleasing flavour. The recipe for Mongolian Lamb is a perfect example.

Cattle are considered too valuable as working animals, and grazing land is scarce, so beef is not common in traditional Chinese dishes. But beef is readily available and popular in western countries, and here the Chinese chefs have adapted it to recipes which are a revelation in flavour and in illustrating how a little meat can go a long way.

Not every dish of exquisitely tender beef served at a Chinese meal is cut from the eye of the fillet – though its melting texture would indicate just that. There is a secret worth knowing. While rump and fillet must be used if there is no time to marinate it, cheaper cuts of lean meat may be used for stir-fried dishes if they are tenderized in this way.

Use round, blade or skirt steak, and freeze it until just firm enough to slice very thinly. For 450 g (1 lb) of meat, dissolve 2.5 ml (½ tsp) bicarbonate of soda in 60 ml (4 tbsp) of water. Add this to the meat and knead well until liquid is absorbed. Refrigerate for at least 2 hours, or overnight if possible. Proceed with the recipe. If liked, other marinade ingredients may be added along with the tenderizing marinade. This method is used in many Chinese restaurants, making cheaper meat as tender as the choicest fillet.

Left: *clockwise from front: lily buds; preserved kumquats; sliced chilli; Barbecued Pork (see page 110); Cold Steamed Lamb with Pungent Sauce (see page 121); barbecued pork spareribs; Clay Pot Beef (see page 104); lap cheong; fresh coriander; lotus root.*

Clay Pot Beef

Drop the piece of beef into a pan of boiling water and simmer for 5 minutes. Rinse under cold water. Remove excess fat and gristle, and cut the meat into 1.5 cm (½ inch) slices.

Shake the peppercorns in a dry pan over low heat until they smell pungent. Grind to fine powder with a pestle and mortar.

Heat a wok, add 45 ml (3 tbsp) of the oil and fry the meat until brown on all sides.

Place the meat in a clay pot or heatproof bowl and add the pepper, salt, sugar, ginger, garlic, wine, star anise and tangerine peel. Cover with a lid or foil, and place in a large steamer or boiler which contains water about 5 cm (2 inches) deep. Simmer for 2 hours, adding more boiling water as necessary.

Meanwhile, soak mushrooms in hot water to cover for 30 minutes. Drain, squeeze out water. Cut off and discard the mushroom stems and cut the caps into quarters. Cut the spring onions into three or four lengths, discarding some of the green top. Cut the Chinese cabbage into 5 cm (2 inch) lengths.

Heat a wok and add 15 ml (1 tbsp) of the oil. Stir-fry the spring onions and mushrooms for 2 minutes. Then add the meat together with any liquid in the bowl. Remove the star anise and tangerine peel. Add the soy sauce and oyster sauce to the meat, cover the wok and simmer for 10 minutes.

Blanch the cabbage for 1 minute in boiling salted water to which the remaining 15 ml (1 tbsp) of oil has been added. Drain well and add to the meat. Serve with steamed rice.

Note: The finely peeled rind of 1 orange may be used instead of the dried tangerine peel.

Serves 6

900 g (2 lb) brisket of beef or other stewing beef
5 ml (1 tsp) Szechwan peppercorns
75 ml (5 tbsp) oil
2.5 ml (½ tsp) salt
10 ml (2 tsp) sugar
4 slices fresh ginger
2 cloves garlic, peeled
15 ml (1 tbsp) Chinese wine or dry sherry
2 whole star anise
1 piece dried tangerine peel
5 dried Chinese mushrooms
6 spring onions
3–4 stalks Chinese cabbage
15 ml (1 tbsp) dark soy sauce
15 ml (1 tbsp) oyster sauce

Place the beef in a clay pot with flavourings.

Cut Chinese cabbage into pieces.

Add meat and juices to stir-fried vegetables.

Beef in Black Bean Sauce

Serves 4
350 g (12 oz) lean rump or
   fillet steak
15 ml (1 tbsp) canned
   salted black beans
1 large onion
1 head broccoli or 1
   Chinese mustard
   cabbage (gai choy)
10 ml (2 tsp) cornflour
60 ml (4 tbsp) peanut oil
5 ml (1 tsp) crushed garlic
5 ml (1 tsp) finely grated
   fresh ginger
Sauce:
15 ml (1 tbsp) dark soy
   sauce
75 ml (3 fl oz) water or
   stock
5 ml (1 tsp) sugar
5 ml (1 tsp) sesame oil

Cut the broccoli into bite-size pieces.

Cut partially frozen beef into paper-thin slices.

Trim any fat from the beef. Freeze the beef only until firm enough to cut into paper-thin slices. Use a very sharp knife for the slicing.

Put the black beans into a small strainer and rinse under cold water for a few seconds. Drain, and chop them on a wooden board or mash them with a fork.

Peel the onion, cut it in half lengthways and cut each half into six wedges. Cut the broccoli into bite-size pieces, keeping a bit of stem with each floret; or slice the Chinese cabbage into thick pieces. Blanch the green vegetable for 1 minute in boiling salted water; drain.

Mix the cornflour with 15 ml (1 tbsp) of cold water. In another bowl, combine the sauce ingredients.

Heat the wok until very hot, add 30 ml (2 tbsp) of the peanut oil and swirl to coat the cooking surface. Stir-fry the onion for 1 minute. Remove the onion and set it aside with the green vegetables.

Add a further 15 ml (1 tbsp) of peanut oil to the wok and when very hot, stir-fry the beef slices over high heat, tossing and stirring so that all the meat comes into contact with the hot pan and it loses its redness.

Push the meat to one side of the wok, heat the remaining 15 ml (1 tbsp) of peanut oil, add the garlic and ginger and stir for a few seconds until they smell fragrant. Add the black beans and fry, stirring, for a few seconds more. Toss with the meat, add the sauce mixture, reduce the heat and simmer for 2 minutes.

Add the cornflour mixture and stir until the sauce boils and thickens. Add the vegetables and toss together until heated through. Serve immediately with rice.

Seared Fillet Steak in Plum Sauce

Serves 4–6
450 g (1 lb) fillet steak
30 ml (2 tbsp) light soy
   sauce
15 ml (1 tbsp) Chinese
   wine or dry sherry
5 ml (1 tsp) grated ginger
5 ml (1 tsp) sugar
1 clove garlic crushed in
   2.5 ml (½ tsp) salt
1 Chinese chard cabbage
   (bok choy)
peanut oil for deep frying
2.5 ml (½ tsp) sugar
6 spring onions
30 ml (2 tbsp) oil
60 ml (4 tbsp) plum sauce

Trim the beef, removing all fat and gristle. Cut into 1.5 cm (½ inch) slices. Press each slice of meat with the palm of your hand to flatten it slightly. Combine the soy sauce, wine, ginger, sugar and garlic. Add the beef and turn the slices to coat them. Leave to marinate for 1 hour or longer.

Meanwhile prepare the Chinese cabbage. Shred the green leaves of the cabbage very finely. Heat oil in a wok for deep frying and when hot, add the shredded cabbage. Scoop it out with a wire spoon almost immediately. Drain and sprinkle it with the sugar to keep crisp.

Cut the spring onions into 2.5 cm (1 inch) lengths.

Heat a wok, add 15 ml (1 tbsp) of the oil and when hot, fry half of the beef, pressing the slices against the wok and turning to brown both sides. Remove and set aside. Add the remaining 15 ml (1 tbsp) of oil to the wok and when hot, cook the remaining beef. Add the spring onions and first lot of meat and toss together.

Stir in plum sauce and about 15 ml (1 tbsp) of water. Cook for about 1 minute until thoroughly heated. Serve on a bed of crisp-fried Chinese cabbage.

Cut beef into thick slices.

Briefly fry Chinese cabbage until crisp.

Slice spring onions diagonally.

Shredded Beef with Asparagus

Serves 3–4
350 g (12 oz) lean steak
2.5 ml (½ tsp) bicarbonate
  of soda
2 onions
1 bunch asparagus
75 ml (5 tbsp) peanut oil
Marinade:
10 ml (2 tsp) dark soy
  sauce
10 ml (2 tsp) cornflour
2.5 ml (½ tsp) sugar
15 ml (1 tbsp) Chinese
  wine or dry sherry
Sauce:
15 ml (1 tbsp) light soy
  sauce
15 ml (1 tbsp) bottled
  oyster sauce
15 ml (1 tbsp) water
10 ml (2 tsp) cornflour

Cut the meat into fine shreds, discarding any fat. Dissolve the bicarbonate of soda in 60 ml (4 tbsp) of water, pour this over the meat and knead well until the meat absorbs the liquid. Refrigerate for 2 hours or longer if possible. This tenderizes economical cuts of meat. If time is short, use a tender cut of beef and omit this step.

Peel the onions and cut them in half lengthways, then cut each half into six wedges. Snap off any tough ends of asparagus and discard; cut the stalks into 5 cm (2 inch) lengths.

Combine the marinade ingredients, add to the meat and mix well. Leave to marinate for about 20 minutes. In a small bowl, mix the sauce ingredients.

Heat a wok, add 30 ml (2 tbsp) of the peanut oil and stir-fry the onions over high heat for 1 minute. Remove the onions to a plate.

Add 30 ml (2 tbsp) of peanut oil to the wok and when very hot, add the meat and toss over high heat until its colour changes. Put the meat aside with the onions.

Wipe out the wok and heat the remaining 15 ml (1 tbsp) of peanut oil. Stir-fry the asparagus for 1 minute. Then add 50 ml (2 fl oz) hot water, cover the wok and cook for 3 minutes or until the asparagus is tender but still crisp.

Add the sauce ingredients and stir until boiling and slightly thickened. Then return the beef and onions to the wok and toss together until heated through. Serve hot.

Snap off ends of asparagus.

Stir-fry shredded beef until it changes colour.

Add hot water to stir-fried asparagus.

Chilli Beef with Bitter Melon

Bitter melon

Halve bitter melon and scoop out spongy centre.

Rinse black beans under cold water.

Remove any fat from the meat and slice the meat thinly across the grain. Dissolve the bicarbonate of soda in 60 ml (4 tbsp) of hot water. Add to the meat and knead well until the meat absorbs all the liquid. Cover and refrigerate for 2 hours or longer.

Halve the bitter melon lengthways. Scoop out and discard the spongy centre and seeds. Cut the melon into 12 mm (½ inch) slices. Sprinkle 5 ml (1 tsp) of salt over the melon pieces and lightly mix through. Leave for 30 minutes or longer.

Rinse the melon pieces under a cold tap, and drain. Rinse the black beans under cold water, drain, and chop. Combine the soy sauce, chilli bean sauce, sugar and cornflour with 75 ml (5 tbsp) of water.

Heat the wok, add 45 ml (3 tbsp) of the oil and when hot, add the beef and stir-fry over high heat, tossing and stirring until brown. Remove to a plate.

Add a further 15 ml (1 tbsp) of oil to the wok and when hot, stir-fry the bitter melon for 2 minutes. Remove.

Heat the remaining oil, add garlic and stir-fry for a few seconds. Add black beans and fry, stirring for a few seconds more. Stir the sauce mixture, add it to the wok and stir until it boils and thickens. Return the melon to the wok, simmer for 5 minutes. Then stir in the beef until reheated through. Serve immediately, garnished with chilli flowers.

Serves 4
- 350 g (12 oz) piece of chuck or skirt steak
- 2.5 ml (½ tsp) bicarbonate of soda
- 1 large bitter melon
- 5 ml (1 tsp) salt
- 15 ml (1 tbsp) canned Chinese salted black beans
- 15 ml (1 tbsp) dark soy sauce
- 10 ml (2 tsp) chilli bean sauce
- 5 ml (1 tsp) sugar
- 5 ml (1 tsp) cornflour
- 90 ml (6 tbsp) peanut oil
- 5 ml (1 tsp) crushed garlic

Stir-Fried Beef with Peppers

Serves 4–6

450 g (1 lb) beef fillet or rump
1 clove garlic
5 ml (1 tsp) salt
5 ml (1 tsp) finely grated fresh ginger
2.5 ml (½ tsp) five spice powder
1 large red pepper
1 large green pepper
10 ml (2 tsp) cornflour
75 ml (5 tbsp) cold water
30 ml (2 tbsp) dark soy sauce
10 ml (2 tsp) sesame oil
30 ml (2 tbsp) peanut oil

Trim off all fat from the beef. Place it in the freezer for about 2 hours, long enough to make it firm, not hard. This makes it easy to cut into paper-thin slices.

Crush garlic with salt, and rub into beef with the ginger and five spice, mixing well.

Remove stem, seeds and membranes from the red and green peppers and cut into thin slices. In a small bowl, mix the cornflour, water, soy sauce and sesame oil together.

Heat a wok and when hot, add 15 ml (1 tbsp) of the peanut oil and heat for a further 30 seconds. Swirl the wok to coat its inner surface. Add the pepper strips and stir-fry over high heat for 1 minute. Remove from wok.

Add the remaining 15 ml (1 tbsp) of peanut oil and heat again, then add the beef and fry over high heat for 2 minutes, stirring constantly, until the beef changes colour. Add the cornflour mixture and stir until it boils and thickens. Then return the pepper strips to the wok and combine with beef.

Serve immediately accompanied by rice or noodles.

Slice partially frozen beef thinly.

Barbecued Pork

Special barrel-shaped ovens are used to cook this popular item. This recipe gives two ways to get almost the same effect in your own oven at home.

Cut the pork lengthways into three or four strips. Crush the garlic with the salt and combine with all the remaining ingredients in a large bowl. Add the pork and mix well together so that the meat is covered on all sides with the mixture. Allow it to marinate for 15 minutes or longer if convenient.

For the first cooking method, the pork is hung in strips from the top rack in the oven. To make suitable hooks, cut lengths of wire 10 cm (4 inches) long from wire coat-hangers using pliers or wire cutters. Shape each end into an 'S' shape, the top hook smaller than the base which holds the pork.

Remove all racks from oven except one, which should be on the highest level. Put a roasting pan with a little water in it on the bottom shelf.

Preheat the oven to 200°C (400°F) mark 6. Insert a metal hook in the end of each strip of pork and hang it from the rack. Roast for 15 minutes in the hot oven, then reduce the temperature to 190°C (375°F) mark 5, brush the meat with the marinade and continue roasting for a further 30 minutes or until the pork is cooked.

Remove from oven, allow to cool for at least 10 minutes, then cut in thin slices crossways.

The second method of cooking is to half-fill a roasting pan with hot water and put a wire rack across the top of the pan. Place the strips of pork on the rack (reserving the marinade) and roast in an oven preheated to 200°C (400°F) mark 6 for 15 minutes, then turn the pork, brush with marinade and continue roasting for 15 minutes. Turn the meat again and baste it, and roast for another 15 minutes or until the pork is tender and well glazed.

Barbecued pork may be served hot or cold as an hors d'oeuvre or part of a meal, or the meat can be used in other dishes such as fried rice. Stir-fried with mange-tout or fresh green beans, it makes a quick, light meal. On its own, serve with plum sauce and steamed bread.

Thread pork on wire hooks.

To cook, hang from shelf in oven.

Or place the strips on a wire rack in a roasting pan.

Serves 4–6
900 g (2 lb) pork fillet or tenderloin
5 ml (1 tsp) finely chopped garlic
5 ml (1 tsp) salt
2.5 ml (½ tsp) finely grated fresh ginger
30 ml (2 tbsp) dark soy sauce
30 ml (2 tbsp) honey
30 ml (1 tbsp) Chinese wine or dry sherry
2.5 ml (½ tsp) five spice powder
15 ml (1 tbsp) bottled hoi sin sauce

Stir-Fried Garlic Beef and Mustard Cabbage

Remove any fat from the meat. Slice the meat thinly across the grain.

In a bowl, dissolve the bicarbonate of soda in 75 ml (5 tbsp) of water. Add the sugar, cornflour and sliced meat and knead the liquid well into the meat until the liquid is absorbed. Refrigerate for 2 hours or overnight.

Soak the mushrooms in hot water for 30 minutes. Discard the mushroom stems, and cut the caps into halves (or quarters, if large).

Wash the cabbage and drain it well, then slice diagonally, discarding any tough ends of outer leaves.

Crush the garlic in the salt. Combine the ingredients for the sauce in a small bowl.

Heat a wok, add 45 ml (3 tbsp) of the peanut oil and swirl the wok to coat its sides. Add beef and stir-fry over high heat until the meat's colour changes. Remove to a plate.

Add the remaining 15 ml (1 tbsp) of peanut oil to the wok. When hot add the cabbage, garlic and mushrooms, and stir-fry for 1 minute. Then return the meat to the wok and continue to cook for 30 seconds. Add the sauce mixture and stir through. Turn off the heat and stir in the sesame oil. Serve immediately with boiled rice.

Serves 3–4

350 g (12 oz) skirt steak
2.5 ml (½ tsp) bicarbonate of soda
5 ml (1 tsp) sugar
5 ml (1 tsp) cornflour
6–8 dried Chinese mushrooms
1 small bunch Chinese mustard cabbage (gai choy), about 225 g (8 oz)
4 cloves garlic
5 ml (1 tsp) salt
60 ml (4 tbsp) peanut oil
10 ml (2 tsp) sesame oil
Sauce:
15 ml (1 tbsp) Chinese wine or dry sherry
15 ml (1 tbsp) dark soy sauce
30 ml (2 tbsp) oyster sauce

Work the bicarbonate of soda mixture into the meat to tenderize.

Crush the garlic with salt.

Stir-fry cabbage, garlic and mushrooms.

Braised Pork Spareribs with Smoked Mussels

Serves 4–6
700 g (1½ lb) pork spare-
   ribs
2 cloves garlic, crushed
15 ml (1 tbsp) light soy
   sauce
15 ml (1 tbsp) Chinese
   wine or dry sherry
2.5 ml (½ tsp) salt
30 ml (2 tbsp) peanut oil
450 ml (¾ pint) hot stock
   or water
100 g (4 oz) canned
   smoked mussels
15 ml (1 tbsp) cornflour

Cut the spareribs into chunky pieces. Mix together the
garlic, soy sauce, wine and salt, and marinate the spareribs in this mixture for at least 30 minutes.

Heat a wok and when very hot, add the oil and swirl to
coat the surface. On high heat, fry the spareribs, tossing
to brown all surfaces. Turn the heat to low, add the hot
stock (or water) and 2 or 3 mussels to give a pronounced
smoky flavour. Cover the wok and simmer for 45 minutes
or until the pork is tender and the liquid reduced.

Add the remaining mussels and cook for a further 10
minutes.

Blend the cornflour smoothly with 15 ml (1 tbsp) of
cold water, add this to the wok and stir constantly until
the sauce boils and thickens. Serve hot with rice.

*Cut spareribs into chunky
pieces.*

Add mussels to spareribs.

Mu Shu Pork

Serves 4
225 g (8 oz) boneless lean
  pork
10 ml (2 tsp) light soy
  sauce
10 ml (2 tsp) Chinese wine
  or dry sherry
10 ml (2 tsp) cornflour
4 dried Chinese
  mushrooms
30 dried lily buds
30 ml (2 tbsp) dried wood
  fungus (cloud ears)
1 piece canned winter
  bamboo shoot
2 spring onions
1 whole egg and 1 egg yolk
2.5 ml (½ tsp) salt

45 ml (3 tbsp) peanut oil
5 ml (1 tsp) sesame oil
Sauce:
15 ml (1 tbsp) oyster sauce
15 ml (1 tbsp) Chinese
  wine or dry sherry
15 ml (1 tbsp) light soy
  sauce
For serving:
hoi sin or sweet chilli
  sauce
spring onion tassels
Mandarin Pancakes (see
  page 141), or Silver
  Thread Rolls (page 142),
  or Flower Rolls (page
  143)

Fun to eat, this is something you use your fingers for like Crisp-Fried Boneless Duck or Lettuce Rolls. Brush each pancake with hoi sin or sweet chilli sauce, top with some pork filling, roll up and enjoy. Serve as a first course or a complete light luncheon.

Partially freeze the pork until it is firm enough to cut into very thin slices, then into shreds. Use a very sharp knife for slicing. Mix with the soy sauce, wine and 5 ml (1 tsp) of the cornflour. Refrigerate for at least 30 minutes.

Meanwhile, put the dried mushrooms and lily buds into a bowl, pour very hot water to cover them, and soak for 30 minutes. Then drain, discard the mushroom stems and cut the mushroom caps into thin strips. Discard the hard tips of the lily buds and tie each bud into a knot.

Soak the wood fungus in cold water for 10 minutes. Drain, pinch off any hard, gritty portions and cut the shapes into smaller pieces.

Shred the bamboo shoot into matchstick strips. Finely slice the spring onions. Combine the sauce ingredients with 60 ml (4 tbsp) of water. Beat the egg and yolk together with the salt.

Heat a wok, add 15 ml (1 tbsp) of the peanut oil and pour in the beaten egg. Swirl the pan, then stir and cook until the egg is firm without browning. Remove from heat and cut into small pieces with a wok chan. Immediately turn out onto a dish. Wipe the wok with absorbent kitchen paper.

Reheat the wok, add another 15 ml (1 tbsp) of peanut oil and stir-fry the bamboo shoot and spring onions on high heat for 1 minute. Remove to plate.

Heat the remaining 15 ml (1 tbsp) of peanut oil. On high heat, stir-fry the pork, mushrooms and lily buds until the pork changes colour. Add the sauce mixture, cover the wok and cook for 3 minutes. Mix the remaining 5 ml (1 tsp) of cornflour with 15 ml (1 tbsp) of cold water and stir into the sauce until it boils and thickens.

Return the spring onions and bamboo shoot to the wok, together with the wood fungus. Drizzle the sesame oil over and stir rapidly together. Remove from heat and fold in the cooked egg.

Serve hot with spring onion tassels and either Mandarin Pancakes, Silver Thread Rolls, or Flower Rolls.

Cut pork into shreds.

Tie lily buds into knots.

Stir-Fried Pork with Walnuts and Lotus Root

Thinly slice partially frozen pork.

Slice lotus root.

Walnut skins lift off easily after boiling.

Serves 4

350 g (12 oz) pork fillet or escalopes
10 ml (2 tsp) light soy sauce
5 ml (1 tsp) Chinese wine or dry sherry
2.5 ml (½ tsp) salt
2.5 ml (½ tsp) crushed garlic
2.5 ml (½ tsp) finely grated fresh ginger
1 canned lotus root
50 g (2 oz) peeled walnut halves
oil for frying
10 ml (2 tsp) cornflour
Sauce:
125 ml (4 fl oz) stock or water
10 ml (2 tsp) bottled oyster sauce
15 ml (1 tbsp) Chinese wine or dry sherry
5 ml (1 tsp) sesame oil
5 ml (1 tsp) chilli oil (optional)

Freeze the pork until it is firm enough to cut into paper-thin slices. Use a very sharp knife for the slicing.

Combine the soy sauce, wine, salt, garlic, and ginger in a bowl. Add the sliced pork, mix well and leave to marinate.

Slice the lotus root thinly and set aside. Peeled walnuts are not always easy to find, but it is better to remove the fine skin as this becomes bitter when the walnuts are fried. Here is an easy way to do this. Bring a small pan of water to the boil, add the walnut halves and simmer for 7 minutes. Drain, then spread on absorbent kitchen paper. The thin skin may be peeled off easily.

Heat about 250 ml (8 fl oz) oil in a wok and deep fry the nuts on low heat, stirring and turning them constantly, just until golden brown (this should take less than a minute). Drain on absorbent kitchen paper.

Mix all the sauce ingredients together.

Reheat the wok, add 15 ml (1 tbsp) of oil and swirl to coat the wok. When the oil is very hot, add the marinated pork mixture and stir-fry on high heat until the pork is browned. Add the sauce mixture and when it boils lower the heat, cover the wok and simmer for 5 minutes.

Blend the cornflour with 15 ml (1 tbsp) of cold water, stir this in to the pork mixture. When the sauce boils and thickens slightly, add the lotus root and heat through. Arrange on a dish and sprinkle the walnut halves over. Garnish with cucumber.

Pork with Sweet Cumquats

Serves 4

350 g (12 oz) pork fillet or
 lean pork chops, boned
15 ml (1 tbsp) Chinese
 wine or dry sherry
15 ml (1 tbsp) light soy
 sauce
5 ml (1 tsp) grated fresh
 ginger
15 ml (1 tbsp) cornflour
3 spring onions
peanut oil for deep frying
8 sweet kumquats pre-
 served in syrup
Sauce:
15 ml (2 tbsp) Chinese
 wine or dry sherry
15 ml (1 tbsp) sugar
15 ml (1 tbsp) light soy
 sauce
30 ml (2 tbsp) white
 vinegar
15 ml (1 tbsp) kumquat
 syrup
5 ml (1 tsp) cornflour

Cut the pork into small squares. Marinate in wine, soy sauce and ginger for 20 minutes.

Stir the cornflour into the pork and marinade. Cut the spring onions diagonally into short lengths. Combine the sauce ingredients with 15 ml (1 tbsp) of water.

Heat a wok, add oil for deep frying and when hot, fry the pork in three or four batches until brown and cooked through. Drain. Pour the oil from the wok into a heat-proof bowl and reserve for future use.

Return 15 ml (1 tbsp) of the oil to the wok and gently cook the spring onions. Add the pork and sauce mixture, stirring constantly until heated through. Lastly stir in the kumquats. Serve immediately on a bed of Stir-Fried Lettuce (see page 49).

Cumquats in syrup.

Cut the pork into pieces.

Deep fry the pork in 3 or 4 batches.

Braised Honey Pork

Serves 6

900 g (2 lb) boneless loin of pork
15 ml (1 tbsp) canned black beans
5 ml (1 tsp) crushed garlic
5 ml (1 tsp) salt
10 ml (2 tsp) finely grated fresh ginger
45 ml (3 tbsp) honey
45 ml (3 tbsp) Chinese wine or dry sherry
2.5 ml (½ tsp) five spice powder
60 ml (4 tbsp) dark soy sauce
45 ml (3 tbsp) peanut oil

Ask the butcher to remove rind from the pork. Cut the pork into strips 5 cm × 2.5 cm (2 inches × 1 inch).

Wash the black beans well under running cold water. Drain and chop. Combine all ingredients except the peanut oil and mix with the pork. Leave for at least 15 minutes to marinate.

Heat a wok, add the peanut oil and swirl to coat the wok. Add the pork pieces (reserving the marinade) and stir-fry until they are browned. Then add the reserved marinade. Swirl 175 ml (6 fl oz) hot water in the marinating bowl and add that too.

Reduce the heat, cover the wok and simmer for 30 to 40 minutes until pork is tender. Stir occasionally and add more hot water if the liquid seems to be drying up. Be careful that the sweet marinade does not burn. The heat should be very low throughout the cooking.

When the pork is tender, remove from heat. If it is not to be served straightaway, it may be reheated at serving time. Serve on a bed of Braised Chinese Cabbage (see page 48) with plain rice and garnish with coriander.

Cut the pork into strips.

Stir-fry the marinated pork until brown.

Spicy Pork Spareribs

Serves 6–8

1.4 kg (3 lb) rack of
 Chinese-style pork
 spareribs
7.5 ml (1½ tsp) crushed
 garlic
5 ml (1 tsp) sugar
5 ml (1 tsp) finely grated
 fresh ginger
45 ml (3 tbsp) dark soy
 sauce
15 ml (1 tbsp) bottled hoi
 sin sauce
10 ml (2 tsp) sesame sauce
15 ml (1 tbsp) honey
5–10 ml (1–2 tsp) chilli
 sauce (optional)
15 ml (1 tbsp) Chinese
 wine or dry sherry

Ask the butcher to cut rack of bones into lengths of four or five bones each. At home, use a sharp knife to cut between the bones, but do not separate them.

Crush the garlic with the sugar and combine with all the remaining ingredients in a large bowl. Beat well with a spoon to mix together. The sesame sauce should be stirred well in its jar before measuring the required amount, because the oil will have floated to the top and the paste will be settled at the bottom. Pour the marinade over the pork and rub it in on all sides and between the bones. Marinate for 1 hour or more.

Preheat the oven to 200°C (400°F) mark 6. Place a rack in a roasting pan (or across the top) and pour some hot water into the pan; water should not touch the rack. Place the marinated spareribs on the rack. Cook in the hot oven for 20 minutes, then reduce the temperature to 180°C (350°F) mark 4, turn the ribs over and cook for a further 25 minutes or longer.

When ready, the spareribs should be reddish-brown all over, touched with dark brown here and there as if barbe-cued over open coals. Depending on thickness of the spareribs, the total cooking time may be between 45 minutes and 1 hour. Cut into pieces to serve and garnish with tomato roses and coriander.

This dish can be cooked ahead and reheated under the griller.

Note: The spareribs can also be cooked in a frying pan. Heat 15–30 ml (1–2 tbsp) of peanut oil in a large, heavy frying pan and brown them. Add 125 ml (4 fl oz) hot water, cover the frying pan and simmer for 30 to 35 minutes or until tender. Then cook, uncovered, until liquid evaporates and the ribs look glazed.

Make cuts between the ribs.

Rub marinade over ribs.

Place ribs on a rack over water for baking.

Stir-Fried Lamb with Chilli and Garlic

Add lamb to soy mixture.

Slice water chestnuts.

Garlic is combined with chilli bean sauce.

Serves 6

450 g (1 lb) leg steaks (or shoulder chops)

15 ml (1 tbsp) light soy sauce

10 ml (2 tsp) grated fresh ginger

10 ml (2 tsp) cornflour

15 ml (1 tbsp) Chinese wine or dry sherry

5 ml (1 tsp) sugar

3 spring onions

225 g (8 oz) can water chestnuts

100 g (4 oz) mange-tout

10 ml (2 tsp) crushed garlic

10 ml (2 tsp) bottled chilli bean sauce

75 ml (5 tbsp) peanut oil

Sauce:

30 ml (2 tbsp) dark soy sauce

15 ml (1 tbsp) sugar

15 ml (1 tbsp) Chinese wine or dry sherry

10 ml (2 tsp) cornflour

10 ml (2 tsp) Chinese black vinegar

60 ml (4 tbsp) water

Trim and discard the skin, fat and bones from the steaks. Cut the meat into strips. Combine the soy sauce, ginger, cornflour, wine and sugar. Add the lamb strips and mix well. Leave to marinate for 30 minutes.

Finely chop the spring onions. Drain the water chestnuts and halve them. Combine the sauce ingredients in a small bowl. String and wash the mange-tout. Combine the garlic and the chilli bean sauce.

Heat a wok until very hot. Add 60 ml (4 tbsp) of the peanut oil and swirl to coat the wok. Add the lamb and stir-fry over high heat until the meat changes colour. Add the spring onion, water chestnuts and mange-tout, and fry for about 30 seconds.

Push the meat and vegetables to one side of the wok, add the remaining 15 ml (1 tbsp) of peanut oil in the centre, and fry the garlic and chilli bean sauce, stirring, for a few seconds until it smells fragrant.

Stir the sauce ingredients again because the cornflour will have settled at the bottom, add this to the wok and stir until the sauce is thick and clear. Toss the meat and vegetables in the sauce, and serve at once. Garnish with sliced cucumber and onion flowers.

Sesame Lamb on Crisp Noodles

Trim all the fat from the lamb and remove the bones. Cut the meat into very thin slices. Mix with the sugar, salt and soy sauce. Leave for 10 minutes.

Add the egg white, 15 ml (1 tbsp) of peanut oil and the cornflour. Mix well and chill for 30 minutes.

Cut the spring onions into bite-sized pieces. Slice the pepper into strips.

Heat a wok, add 45 ml (3 tbsp) of peanut oil. When hot, add the garlic, spring onions and pepper, and stir-fry for 10 seconds. Then add the meat and stir-fry until its colour changes. Remove and set aside.

Add all ingredients for the sauce to the wok, add 45 ml (3 tbsp) of water and stir over low heat until it is smooth. Return the lamb and vegetables to the wok and stir until heated. Serve on a bed of fried noodles.

To prepare the noodles: Heat 350 ml (12 fl oz) of peanut oil in a wok and when hot, add about one-quarter of the noodles at a time. They will puff and turn white instantly. Drain on absorbent kitchen paper. They may be done beforehand, but store them in an airtight container until served.

Serves 4
450 g (1 lb) lean lamb
  chops
5 ml (1 tsp) sugar
2.5 ml (½ tsp) salt
15 ml (1 tbsp) light soy
  sauce
1 egg white
peanut oil
10 ml (2 tsp) cornflour
3 spring onions
1 small red pepper
2.5 ml (½ tsp) crushed
garlic
50 g (2 oz) bean starch
  (transparent) noodles or
  rice vermicelli
Sauce:
20 ml (4 tsp) sesame sauce
45 ml (3 tbsp) dark soy
  sauce
45 ml (3 tbsp) Chinese
  wine or dry sherry
5 ml (1 tsp) sugar
2.5 ml (½ tsp) chilli oil
  (optional)

Stir-fry garlic, spring onions, pepper and lamb.

The transparent noodles.

Noodles puff and turn white instantly when fried.

Mongolian Lamb

Serves 4

450 g (1 lb) boned leg of lamb
10 ml (2 tsp) sugar
5 ml (1 tsp) salt
30 ml (2 tbsp) dark soy sauce
1 small egg, beaten
2.5 ml (½ tsp) bicarbonate of soda
10 ml (2 tsp) cornflour
75 ml (5 tbsp) peanut oil
1 large onion cut in wedges lengthways
1 spring onion, finely sliced
5 ml (1 tsp) finely chopped garlic

Sauce:
1.25 ml (¼ tsp) five spice powder
15 ml (1 tbsp) bottled hoi sin sauce
15 ml (1 tbsp) bottled ground bean sauce (mor sze jeung)
5 ml (1 tsp) chilli bean sauce
15 ml (1 tbsp) Chinese wine or dry sherry

The process of soaking, rinsing and marinating lessens the strong flavour of lamb, which is not popular in China except in the north. It also tenderizes the meat. This recipe uses about half a small leg of lamb – the rest may be used for another dish or frozen.

Trim away any fat, skin and gristle from the meat. Freeze the meat until firm, then cut into bite-size, paper-thin slices. Soak in cold water for 30 minutes. Rinse under a cold tap until water runs clear, then drain well and squeeze out excess water.

Combine the sugar, salt, soy sauce, egg, bicarbonate of soda and cornflour. Add the meat and mix well. Add 15 ml (1 tbsp) of the peanut oil and mix again. Leave to marinate for at least 2 hours.

Heat a wok, add 15 ml (1 tbsp) of the peanut oil and, on medium-high heat, stir-fry the onion wedges and spring onion for 1 minute. Remove from the wok.

Add the remaining 45 ml (3 tbsp) of peanut oil to the wok, heat the oil and swirl to coat the cooking surface. Fry the garlic for 5 seconds. Then add the lamb and stir-fry on high heat, tossing the meat constantly until it is brown. Add sauce ingredients except the wine, and toss again. Return the onion and spring onion to the wok. Add the wine, pouring it down the sides of the wok so that it sizzles. Mix, and serve at once with rice.

Note: Mongolian lamb is usually cooked on a flat griddle but can be done in the wok. A popular way of presenting this dish in restaurants is on a heated sizzle plate brought to the table.

Slice partially frozen lamb thinly.

Cut onions lengthways into wedges.

Cold Steamed Lamb with Pungent Sauce

Ask the butcher to bone the lamb shoulder, but not roll the meat.

Combine the bean sauce, soy sauce, spring onions, garlic, ginger, star anise broken into pieces, wine, sugar and bean curd. Place the lamb in a bowl that will fit in your steamer, pour the sauce mixture over the lamb and rub it well into the meat. Leave for 30 minutes.

Cover and steam for 1½ hours, adding more boiling water to the steamer to replace the water that boils away.

Pour the liquid from the lamb into a saucepan and simmer until reduced and syrupy. Pour it over the lamb and chill.

To serve, cut the meat into thin slices and arrange them on a platter. It may be served as a part of an hors d'oeuvre selection, or as a cold meat dish accompanied by warm Silver Thread Rolls (see page 142) or Flower Rolls (see page 143).

Note: This dish is also delicious hot. If serving hot, lift the lamb out of the steamer and slice it. Reduce the sauce by quick cooking, then spoon it over the lamb, and serve.

Serves 6

1.1 kg (2½ lb) lamb shoulder, boned
15 ml (1 tbsp) ground bean sauce (mor sze jeung)
45 ml (3 tbsp) dark soy sauce
2 spring onions chopped
5 ml (1 tsp) finely grated garlic
5 ml (1 tsp) finely grated fresh ginger
1 star anise
15 ml (1 tbsp) Chinese wine or dry sherry
15 ml (1 tbsp) sugar
5 ml (1 tsp) red bean curd

The ground bean sauce (mor sze jeung).

Break star anise into pieces.

Place marinated lamb into steamer for cooking.

Rice and Noodles

Whatever else is on the table, rice or noodles are what fill the gaps. No Chinese meal is complete without one or the other, or both.

In the west we have been taught to expect well-cooked rice to be fluffy, so most restaurants serve long-grain rice which gives this result. To most Chinese, however, the medium grain is preferable. When correctly cooked, it is not fluffy but certainly not gluey. Each perfectly cooked grain is pearly and well defined, clinging in friendly fashion to neighbouring grains. Thus it is much easier to pick up with chopsticks, although the shovelling method (bowl held close to the mouth, and chopsticks working furiously) is also perfectly acceptable around the Chinese table.

Short and long-grain rice are not interchangeable in recipes, because the absorption rates are different (long-grain rice requiring more water). The other type of rice sold in Chinese stores, glutinous rice, is used only for moulded snacks or for sweets.

It is not necessary to wash the clean rice sold in most western countries unless there is a lot of loose starch. If washing rice, drain it well afterwards.

In the north of China where wheat grows more readily, noodles, buns and pancakes take the place of rice. In the south, they make noodles from rice flour.

Left: *clockwise from top left: Hokkien noodles; egg noodles; bundle of bean starch noodles; cellophane noodles; bundles of egg noodles; rice vermicelli; twin rice noodles; rice.*

Chinese-Style Steamed Rice

Short or medium-grain rice is most used in China, but in western countries long-grain rice is popular. If using long-grain rice, increase the water to 850 ml (1½ pints) for 450 g (1 lb) rice as it has a greater absorbency.

Wash the rice and drain well, then put the measured water (hot or cold, it does not matter) into a saucepan with the rice.

Bring to the boil over high heat, and boil rapidly for 1 minute. Then reduce the heat to medium, and cook uncovered for 2 to 3 minutes, until holes appear in the rice mass and the surface looks dimpled. Do not stir.

Cover the saucepan with a well-fitting lid, reduce the heat to as low as possible and cook for a further 10 minutes. Without removing the lid, turn off the heat and let the rice sit undisturbed for a further 10 minutes.

Grains will be well defined and separate, but will cling together instead of being fluffy. This makes it easy to eat with chopsticks.

Cook rice, uncovered, until holes appear in the rice mass.

Serves 6
450 g (1 lb) medium-grain rice
700 ml (1¼ pints) water

Vegetarian Fried Rice

Use a mixture of colourful and crisp vegetables in season, diced or finely sliced – green beans, carrots, celery, courgettes, cabbage, broccoli, cooked or frozen peas. Always include spring onions with their green tops for flavour.

For a more elaborate non-vegetarian version, add diced cooked pork or chicken, steamed and sliced lap cheong, cooked and shelled prawns, chopped ham or bacon. Fry before combining with the vegetables and rice. The bean curd may be omitted.

Cook the rice, then spread it on a lightly oiled baking tray to cool; chill overnight if possible. Dice the bean curd. Lightly beat the eggs, with salt and pepper to taste.

Heat wok, add 15 ml (1 tbsp) of peanut oil; swirl. Pour in the egg mixture, and stir until it is firm. Cut the egg into small pieces with a wok chan then remove from the wok and set aside.

Heat the remaining 60 ml (4 tbsp) of oil and when hot, add the spring onions, garlic and ginger. Fry, stirring, for a few seconds until they smell fragrant. Add bean curd and stir-fry for 1 minute. Add vegetables and stir-fry for a further 1-2 minutes until the vegetables are tender but still crisp.

Add rice; stir and toss to heat through. Sprinkle the soy sauce and sesame oil over, and add the coriander and cooked egg. Toss to mix, and serve immediately.

Cut cooked egg with wok chan.

Add rice to vegetables in wok, toss to heat through.

Serves 4–6

700 g (1½ lb) cooked rice, chilled (275 g (10 oz) raw rice)
2 squares pressed bean curd
2 eggs, lightly beaten
salt and pepper, to taste
75 ml (5 tbsp) peanut oil
3 spring onions, finely chopped
5 ml (1 tsp) finely chopped garlic
5 ml (1 tsp) finely grated fresh ginger
15 ml (1 tbsp) dark soy sauce
225 g (8 oz) diced mixed vegetables
5 ml (1 tsp) sesame oil
60 ml (4 tbsp) fresh coriander leaves, coarsely chopped

Sizzling Rice with Sweet and Sour Seafood

Pouring a hot sauce over freshly fried rice cakes makes them hiss and sizzle, and this is altogether a most colourful and entertaining dish. The rice cakes may be made a day or two ahead and stored in an airtight container, then fried just before serving.

Put the rice into a large saucepan about 25 cm (10 inches) in diameter, add 350 ml (12 fl oz) water and bring to the boil. Boil uncovered until there is no visible liquid when pan is tilted and the surface of the rice looks dimpled; do not stir the rice at all. Turn the heat very low, cover the saucepan and cook for a further 15 minutes. Remove from heat and allow to cool.

Lift the rice out of the saucepan with a spatula. Place it on an oiled oven tray and press it with the heel of your hand to flatten it. Place in a preheated oven at 160°C (325°F) mark 3 for 30 minutes or until dry and the edge feels crisp when touched. Remove from oven, allow to cool, then break it into pieces roughly 5 cm (2 inches) square.

Peel and de-vein the prawns, or if using scallops remove any brown veins. Rinse and dry them thoroughly, and place in a bowl. Sprinkle with salt, add the egg white, and mix through. Sprinkle cornflour and oil over, and mix again. Chill for 30 minutes at least.

Dice the pepper, cut the spring onions into short lengths, thaw the peas, and slice the water chestnuts. All this may be done hours ahead.

Prepare the sauce. Put the tomato ketchup, vinegar, soy sauce, wine and sugar into a saucepan; add 175 ml (6 fl oz) water, and stir over heat to dissolve the sugar. Blend the cornflour with 45 ml (3 tbsp) of cold water, add it to the sauce and stir until mixture boils and thickens. Keep warm.

Heat a wok, add about 700 ml (1¼ pints) of peanut oil and when hot, add the prawns (or scallops), stirring gently, until they turn pink. Drain at once, pouring through a wire strainer into a heatproof bowl. This oil can be used later for frying the rice cakes.

Return the wok to the heat, add 45 ml (3 tbsp) of oil, and when hot, add the pepper and stir-fry for 1 minute. Add spring onions, ginger and garlic and fry for 10 seconds or until fragrant. Add the peas and water chestnuts. Stir all the vegetables into the warm sauce.

Wipe out the wok, return to heat and once more heat the peanut oil for deep frying. When the oil is very hot, fry the rice cakes until crisp and golden. Drain and place in a serving bowl.

Reheat the sauce to boiling, add the prawns, and pour into a heated bowl. Quickly take both bowls to the table and pour the hot sauce over the hot rice cakes so they sizzle and steam. Serve at once into individual bowls, so that the rice cakes will still be crisp when eaten.

Serves 6 with other dishes
225 g (8 oz) short-grain rice
450 g (1 lb) small raw prawns or scallops
2.5 ml (½ tsp) salt
1 egg white
15 ml (1 tbsp) cornflour
15 ml (1 tbsp) peanut oil
1 red pepper (capsicum)
3 or 4 spring onions
50 g (2 oz) frozen peas
10 canned water chestnuts
2.5 ml (½ tsp) finely grated fresh ginger
2.5 ml (½ tsp) crushed garlic
700 ml (1¼ pints) peanut oil for deep frying
Sauce:
60 ml (4 tbsp) tomato ketchup
45 ml (3 tbsp) white vinegar
15 ml (1 tbsp) light soy sauce
15 ml (1 tbsp) Chinese wine or dry sherry
60 ml (4 tbsp) sugar
15 ml (1 tbsp) cornflour

Flatten cooked rice with heel of hand.

Break rice into pieces.

Deep fry rice until golden.

Rice Congee

This is a thin porridge or gruel made by simmering rice with water – the traditional Chinese breakfast. It is filling and easily digested, and can be made interesting and delicious when other ingredients are added, such as chicken, fish, pork, abalone, egg, frogs' legs. A favourite addition is crisp-fried Chinese crullers. I first tasted this breakfast in Singapore, once with fish and another time with pork.

Wash and drain the rice, put it into a saucepan with the water and stock, and bring to the boil. Then reduce the heat, cover the saucepan and simmer for 1 hour or until the rice is very soft.

Meanwhile, remove skin and any bones from the fish fillet, cut into thin slices and mix with the sesame oil, salt and ginger. If using chicken breast, cut into fine shreds and marinate as for the fish.

When porridge is cooked to a thick, creamy consistency, stir in the fish or chicken and cook for 1 minute or just long enough to turn slices white and opaque. Ladle into bowls and let each person choose the accompaniments preferred.

Note: The crisp-fried onions are sometimes available at Chinese stores, being the small purple shallots (or 'red onions' as they are called in Asia), finely sliced and fried until golden brown. If preparing them at home, fry in plenty of oil, stirring constantly. Drain, and save the oil to use as a flavouring in many dishes.

Serves 6
**225 g (8 oz) short or
   medium-grain rice**
1 litre (1¾ pints) water
450 ml (16 fl oz) stock
**salt and white pepper to
   taste**
**350 g (12 oz) haddock
   fillets or chicken breast
   fillets**
10 ml (2 tsp) sesame oil
5 ml (1 tsp) salt
**2.5 ml (½ tsp) finely
   grated ginger**
Accompaniments:
**finely chopped spring
   onions**
**fresh red chillies, seeded
   and sliced**
**finely chopped fresh
   coriander leaves**
light soy sauce
crisp-fried onions

Cut fish into slices.

Stir fish into creamy rice.

Hainan Chicken Rice

This is a meal in itself, as it comprises rice, soup, chicken and dipping sauces.

Wash the chicken. Remove fat from the cavity and cut off and discard the tail and wing tips. Wipe with absorbent kitchen paper, and rub salt within the cavity and all over the bird.

In a saucepan just large enough to hold the chicken, bring to the boil at least 2 litres (3¼ pints) of water. Add the spring onions, celery leaves, peppercorns, sprigs of coriander and 10 ml (2 tsp) of salt.

When the water boils, lower the chicken into the pan breast downwards. Let the water return to the boil, then reduce the heat so that it just simmers; cover the pan tightly and simmer for 25 minutes. Remove from heat and leave chicken in the liquid with the pan still tightly covered for a further 45 minutes to finish the cooking.

While chicken is simmering, wash the rice and leave it to drain in a colander for 1 hour.

Lift out and drain the chicken; reserve the stock for cooking the rice and for the soup. Rub the chicken all over with about 10 ml (2 tsp) of the measured sesame oil. When cool enough to handle, chop into bite-size pieces and reassemble on serving platter. Cover with foil and keep warm.

Heat the remaining sesame oil and the peanut oil in a heavy saucepan with a well-fitting lid and, on medium heat, fry the garlic, ginger and onion, stirring until they are golden (take care they do not burn). Remove 15 ml (1 tbsp) of this cooked oil and reserve it for one of the dipping sauces.

Add the rice to the pan and fry for a minute or two, stirring until the grains are coated with oil. Add 1 litre (1¾ pints) of strained chicken stock, and bring to the boil. Add 10 ml (2 tsp) of salt and stir well; then turn the heat very low, cover the saucepan tightly and cook for 15 minutes without lifting the lid. Remove from heat and allow to stand, covered, for a further 10 minutes.

Sauces: For one dipping sauce, combine the sliced chilli and the dark soy sauce. For the second dipping sauce, combine ground chilli, grated ginger, and the reserved 15 ml (1 tbsp) of cooked oil. These sauces may be served in individual sauce dishes – the two combinations being kept separate.

Soup: Bring the remaining strained stock to the boil. Add the shredded Chinese cabbage or washed and drained bean sprouts, and light soy to taste; and remove from heat after it has boiled for no longer than 30 seconds. Sprinkle coriander on top and serve in a soup tureen.

Each person takes a bowl of rice and eats it with chicken dipped in one of the sauces. Soup is ladled over the rice as desired, or sipped between mouthfuls of chicken and rice.

Serves 5–6
1.4 kg (3 lb) roasting chicken
salt
2 spring onions
2 sprigs celery leaves
few black peppercorns
few sprigs fresh coriander
450 g (1 lb) long-grain rice
30 ml (2 tbsp) sesame oil
60 ml (4 tbsp) peanut oil
4 cloves garlic, sliced
4 slices fresh ginger
1 onion, sliced
stock from cooking the chicken
Sauces:
2 fresh red chillies, sliced
75 ml (5 tbsp) dark soy sauce
30 ml (2 tbsp) freshly ground red chilli
30 ml (2 tbsp) finely grated fresh ginger
cooked oil from the recipe
Soup:
stock from cooking the chicken
dash of light soy sauce
225 g (8 oz) shredded Chinese cabbage or bean sprouts
30 ml (2 tbsp) finely chopped fresh coriander

Rub sesame oil all over the simmered chicken.

Add washed and dried rice to garlic, ginger and onion.

Stir shredded Chinese cabbage into soup stock.

Steamed Rice Cups with Mixed Meats

Serve 8–12

8 dried Chinese
mushrooms

15 ml (1 tbsp) dark soy
sauce

10 ml (2 tsp) sugar

20 ml (4 tsp) sesame oil

2 lap cheong (Chinese
sausages)

225 g (8 oz) cooked
chicken or barbecued
pork (see page 110)

450 g (1 lb) glutinous rice
or short-grain rice

45 ml (3 tbsp) light soy
sauce

15 ml (1 tbsp) peanut oil

2.5 ml (½ tsp) crushed
garlic

2.5 ml (½ tsp) finely
grated fresh ginger

125 ml (4 fl oz) Master
Sauce (see page 91)

15 ml (1 tbsp) cornflour

Apart from the 'small eats' served in a Chinese breakfast, there are substantial offerings like this. Use rice bowls to mould the rice – or if you wish to make them more dainty, use Chinese tea cups.

Soak the mushrooms in hot water for 30 minutes. Then discard the mushroom stems and slice the caps. Put 175 ml (6 fl oz) of the mushroom soaking liquid into a small saucepan, add the sliced mushrooms, the dark soy sauce, sugar and 10 ml (2 tsp) of the sesame oil. Simmer, covered, for 10 minutes.

Place the lap cheong in a colander, and steam for 10 minutes; when cool enough to handle, cut into thin diagonal slices. Dice the chicken or pork.

Place the rice in a saucepan with 1 litre (1¾ pints) of water. Add the light soy sauce and the remaining 10 ml (2 tsp) of sesame oil. Bring to the boil quickly, then turn heat very low, cover the saucepan and cook for 20 minutes.

In a wok, heat the peanut oil and fry the garlic and ginger until golden. Add the Master Sauce and the mushroom liquid, bring to the boil, and thicken with the cornflour mixed with a little cold water. Add the mushrooms, lap cheong and diced chicken or pork. Heat through. Remove from heat and stir into the rice.

Fill small cups, pressing the rice mixture firmly, then unmould and serve. If prepared beforehand, steam the rice mixture in cups until heated through.

Note: If no Master Sauce is on hand, substitute a sauce made from 50 ml (2 fl oz) of dark soy, 50 ml (2 fl oz) of dry sherry, 5 ml (1 tsp) of sugar, and 5 ml (1 tsp) of sesame oil.

Steam lap cheong.

Cut lap cheong into diagonal slices.

Fill cups with rice mixture and unmould.

Wheat Noodles

Noodles made from wheat flour and eggs are the most popular. Generally sold in 450 g (1 lb) packets, each packet consists of seven or eight bundles. Allow one bundle per person. Unlike rice noodles and bean starch noodles, wheat noodles are always boiled before frying.

Boiled noodles: An important point is that the bundles of noodles must be soaked in hot water for about 10 minutes before dropping them into boiling water. This is not mentioned in the cooking instructions, yet it makes cooking them so much easier. As the bundles soften, the strands separate and the noodles cook evenly, but if they were dropped straight into boiling water the outside would cook while some strands would stick together in tough clumps. If the noodles are loose packed, the soaking is not necessary.

Soak noodles in hot water before boiling.

Bring to the boil a large saucepan of lightly salted water with 15 ml (1 tbsp) of peanut oil added to prevent boiling over. Drain the soaked noodles in a colander and add to the fast-boiling water. When the water returns to the boil, cook fine noodles for 2 to 3 minutes; wide noodles for 4 to 5 minutes. Test frequently and do not overcook. They should be *al dente*.

Run cold water into the pan, drain immediately in a large colander, and run cold water through the noodles to rinse away excess starch and stop the cooking process. Drain thoroughly.

Soft fried noodles: Sprinkle the well-drained noodles with 15 ml (1 tbsp) of peanut oil and 10 ml (2 tsp) of sesame oil, and toss well. Spread them on a large baking tray and allow to dry in the air for about 1 hour.

Heat a wok or large heavy frying pan, and when very hot, add 60 ml (4 tbsp) of peanut oil. When the oil is very hot, coil the noodles into the pan to make a round or oval cake. Reduce the heat to medium, and fry, shaking the pan but not stirring, until the base is golden. Turn the noodles over and fry the other side. If it is necessary to add a little more oil, drizzle the oil down the sides of the wok and allow it to become hot before it reaches the noodles. Cook for a further 5 minutes or until golden, then transfer to serving dish.

Soft fried noodles are ideal for serving as a base with any stir-fried and well-sauced foods, either singly or in combination.

Fresh wheat noodles: It is possible to buy fresh wheat noodles in Chinese stores. They need only the briefest cooking in boiling water before they are used in soups or soft fried. If preferred, they may be steamed over boiling water. Allow 10 minutes steaming time.

Some varieties of wheat noodles – for example, the thick yellow Hokkien noodles – are already cooked and need only to have boiling water poured over them in a colander.

Combination Chow Mein

Serves 4
225 g (8 oz) fine wheat
   noodles
1 chicken breast
100 g (4 oz) barbecued
   pork (see page 110)
100 g (4 oz) bean sprouts
100 g (4 oz) mange-tout
5 ml (1 tsp) crushed garlic
5 ml (1 tsp) finely grated
   fresh ginger
100 g (4 oz) shredded
   Chinese cabbage
6 spring onions in
   bite-size lengths
1 canned winter bamboo
   shoot, cut into strips
peanut oil
Sauce:
175 ml (6 fl oz) stock
45 ml (3 tbsp) light soy
   sauce
45 ml (3 tbsp) oyster sauce
10 ml (2 tsp) sesame oil
15 ml (1 tbsp) cornflour

This dish of soft fried noodles with mixed meats is very popular. Some westernised versions use crisp fried noodles instead, but this isn't correct. The noodles should be chewy and just slightly crisp on the outside when they have been fried.

Cook the noodles as described on page 130. Drain, toss with oil, and spread on a tray to dry.

Skin and bone the chicken breast, and cut the meat into fine shreds. Cut the barbecued pork into narrow strips. Wash and drain the bean sprouts, discard loose skins and pinch off any straggly tails. String the mange-tout. Have all meat and vegetable ingredients ready.

In a bowl, combine the stock, soy sauce, oyster sauce and sesame oil.

Heat a large heavy frying pan and when hot, add 60 ml (4 tbsp) of peanut oil and fry the noodles on medium heat until crisp and golden on one side (about 5 minutes). Turn them and fry their other side. Remove from heat and keep the noodles warm in the frying pan.

Heat a wok, add 45 ml (3 tbsp) of peanut oil and swirl to coat the wok. Add garlic and ginger, and stir for a few seconds. Add the chicken, and stir-fry until the chicken changes colour. Add the pork and vegetables, and toss for a further 2 minutes. Add the mixed sauce ingredients, and bring to the boil.

Mix the cornflour smoothly with 30 ml (2 tbsp) of cold water, add it to the wok and stir until the sauce boils.

Pour over noodles and serve hot.

Spread cooked noodles on a tray to dry.

Cut barbecued pork into narrow strips.

Turn the fried noodles when golden.

Bean Starch Noodles with Pork

Put the noodles in a large bowl, cover with boiling water, then leave for 20 minutes or until soft and transparent. Strain and cut into short lengths with a sharp knife.

Soak the mushrooms in hot water for 30 minutes, squeeze dry, discard stems, dice finely.

Cut the pork into small dice. Mix the wine, soy sauce, salt, stock and cornflour together in a small bowl.

Heat a wok over high heat, add the peanut oil and swirl it around the wok. When the oil is hot, add the pork and mushrooms and stir-fry until cooked and brown. Add the spring onions and ginger, stir for a few seconds; then add the chilli bean sauce and the chopped chilli, and cook over medium heat for a minute or until the mixture looks and smells cooked.

Add the seasonings and sauce mixture, and stir until it comes to the boil. Then add the noodles and simmer, stirring, until all the liquid has cooked down. Stir in the coriander leaves and serve at once.

If desired, garnish with a chilli flower and extra coriander leaves.

Bean Starch Noodles

Transparent bean starch noodles: these fine noodles are also known as cellophane noodles, bean threads, silver threads, spring rain noodles, harusame or fenszu. For a crisp garnish, fry in the same way as rice vermicelli, straight from the packet. For use in soups or braised dishes, soak in hot water or cook in boiling water for 15 minutes or until tender.

Bean starch is also available in large round **sheets**. These bean sheets consist of a mung bean flour and water paste which has been rolled into thin sheets and dried, ready for use. Soak, cut into strips, and cook in boiling water as directed in recipes.

Serves 4–6
100 g (4 oz) transparent bean starch noodles
6 dried Chinese mushrooms
175 g (6 oz) boneless pork
15 ml (1 tbsp) Chinese wine or dry sherry
15 ml (1 tbsp) light soy sauce
5 ml (1 tsp) salt
175 ml (6 fl oz) light stock
5 ml (1 tsp) cornflour
60 ml (4 tbsp) peanut oil
4 spring onions, finely chopped
10 ml (2 tsp) finely grated fresh ginger
45 ml (3 tbsp) chilli bean sauce
1 large fresh red chilli or red pepper, seeded and finely chopped
60 ml (4 tbsp) chopped fresh coriander leaves

Cover bean starch noodles with boiling water.

Cut into short lengths.

Chop the fresh coriander.

Stir-Fried Noodles, Hokkien Style

Hokkien noodles are thick, yellow wheat noodles sold fresh in Chinese supermarkets, usually in 450 g (1 lb) bags. This mixture of noodles, vegetables and mixed meat and seafood is a one-dish meal.

Pour boiling water over the noodles to cover them, leave for 1 minute, then drain well in a colander.

Steam the lap cheong over simmering water for 5 minutes or until soft. Allow to cool, then cut into slices. If using pork, cut into small dice.

Shell and de-vein the prawns. Clean and slice the squid. Rinse the bean sprouts and pinch off the straggly tails.

Heat a wok, add 60 ml (4 tbsp) oil and swirl to coat. Fry the garlic over low heat until golden. Stir-fry the bean sprouts for a few seconds. Add meat and seafood, and stir-fry until they change colour (about 1 minute). Add noodles, and fry until heated through.

Add soy sauce, vinegar, chilli sauce and stock or water mixed together; and cook, tossing, until the liquid has evaporated. Then remove to a dish.

Rinse the wok, heat it again and when hot, add the remaining 15 ml (1 tbsp) of oil. Pour in the beaten eggs seasoned with salt and pepper; fry quickly, stirring, until firm. Turn off the heat, chop the egg into small pieces with the edge of a wok chan. Return the fried noodle mixture to the wok and toss together. Finally, scatter the garlic chives or spring onions over and serve, garnished with the chillies and celery leaves.

Serves 4

450 g (1 lb) fresh yellow noodles (Hokkien mee)

2 pairs lap cheong (Chinese sausages) or 200 g (7 oz) cooked pork

225 g (8 oz) small prawns, raw or cooked

225 g (8 oz) fresh squid (optional)

225 g (8 oz) fresh bean sprouts

75 ml (5 tbsp) peanut oil

10 ml (2 tsp) finely chopped garlic

45 ml (3 tbsp) dark soy sauce

45 ml (3 tbsp) Chinese white vinegar

45 ml (3 tbsp) sweet chilli sauce

45 ml (3 tbsp) stock or water

salt and pepper to taste

4 eggs, beaten

30 ml (2 tbsp) chopped Chinese garlic chives (koo chye) or green part of spring onions

Garnish:

45 ml (3 tbsp) chopped tender celery leaves

2 fresh red chillies, seeded and sliced

Hokkien noodles.

Add meat and seafood to the stir-fried bean sprouts.

Vegetarian Soup Noodles

Soak the dried mushrooms in hot water for 30 minutes. Discard the mushroom stems, and cut the caps into fine strips; reserve 1.5 litres (2½ pints) of the soaking water (if necessary, make up the quantity with fresh water). Soak the wood fungus in cold water for 10 minutes; then cut into small pieces, trimming off any gritty portions.

Cut the bean curd into small dice or strips. Combine the light soy sauce, sesame oil and sugar, and toss the bean curd in this mixture.

Wash the carrots and cut wedge-shaped sections out of them, lengthways, then slice across to give flower-shapes. String and slice the beans very thinly. String the mange-tout. Cut leaf ribs of the cabbage into bite-size pieces, and finely shred the leaves; keep leaf ribs separate from the shredded leaves. Slice broccoli stems and divide head into florets.

Cook the noodles as described on page 130, drain and divide among six soup bowls.

Heat a wok, add the peanut oil and when hot, fry the chopped spring onions and garlic for a few seconds, stirring, but do not let them darken. Add the mushrooms, the leaf ribs of Chinese cabbage and the broccoli stems and fry for 1 minute longer. Add 1.5 litres (2½ pints) of water including the mushroom soaking water, and the seasoning ingredients; bring to the boil and simmer, covered, for 5 minutes. Add the carrots and beans, and cook for a further 3 minutes. Then add the mange-tout, wood fungus, shredded cabbage leaves and broccoli florets and cook 1 minute longer.

Dissolve the cornflour in 60 ml (4 tbsp) of cold water, and stir it into the soup until it boils and thickens. Drizzle in the beaten egg and stir gently so that it sets in fine shreds. Add the bean curd and heat through. Ladle the soup mixture over the noodles and serve hot.

Serves 6
8 dried Chinese
  mushrooms
45 ml (3 tbsp) dried wood
  fungus (cloud ears)
1 square pressed bean
  curd
45 ml (3 tbsp) light soy
  sauce
10 ml (2 tsp) sesame oil
5 ml (1 tsp) sugar
2 small carrots
12 green beans
100 g (4 oz) mange-tout
8 leaves Chinese cabbage
  (wongah bak)
225 g (8 oz) broccoli
350 g (12 oz) fine egg
  noodles
45 ml (3 tbsp) peanut oil
12 spring onions, chopped
10 ml (2 tsp) finely
  chopped garlic
60 ml (4 tbsp) cornflour
3 eggs, beaten
Seasonings:
45 ml (3 tbsp) light soy
  sauce
60 ml (4 tbsp) Chinese
  wine or dry sherry
10 ml (2 tsp) sesame oil
5 ml (1 tsp) salt
1.25 ml (¼ tsp) ground
  white pepper

Cut the pressed bean curd into small dice.

Cut carrots into flower shapes.

Divide cooked noodles among soup bowls.

Rice Vermicelli with Prawns

Soak the vermicelli for 10 minutes in hot water; drain in a colander. Wash the mustard cabbage, trim off and discard the leaves, and cut the leaf ribs into thin strips. Shell and de-vein the prawns and, if they are large, cut in two lengthways. Mix together the garlic, ginger, wine, oyster sauce, light soy and stock.

Heat a wok, add the peanut oil and swirl to coat the sides of the wok. Add the prawns, stir-fry until they change colour, then transfer them to a bowl containing the sesame oil. Mix thoroughly.

Re-heat the oil in the wok, add the sliced cabbage and stir-fry for 1 minute. Add the mixed liquids and cook for a further 2 minutes.

Add the vermicelli and toss until heated through. Return the prawns to the wok, toss to mix well, and serve immediately.

Serves 4
225 g (8 oz) rice vermicelli
6 leaves mustard cabbage
  (gai choy)
450 g (1 lb) raw prawns
1 clove garlic, crushed
5 ml (1 tsp) finely grated
  fresh ginger
15 ml (1 tbsp) Chinese
  wine or dry sherry
5 ml (1 tsp) oyster sauce
15 ml (1 tbsp) light soy
  sauce
125 ml (4 fl oz) stock
salt to taste
60 ml (4 tbsp) peanut oil
5 ml (1 tsp) sesame oil

Soak vermicelli in hot water.

Cut mustard cabbage into strips.

Rice Noodles

Fresh rice noodles: Sa ho fun and chee cheong fun are sheets of fresh rice noodles which are sliced into strips, then heated by pouring boiling water over them. Drain, then stir-fry with other ingredients or simply serve with a sauce.

Dried rice noodles: There are various kinds of dried rice noodles and, depending on the variety, many have to be soaked in cold water for 30 minutes or longer. Drain, drop into fast-boiling water, and boil for 6 to 10 minutes, testing frequently. As soon as they are tender, drain in a colander, and rinse well in cold running water so that they cannot continue to cook in their own heat. Drain once more. Fry or heat in soup before serving.

Dried rice vermicelli: Rice vermicelli has very fine strands and cooks very quickly. Depending on the recipe, they should be cooked in boiling water for 2 minutes or else soaked in hot water. Drain well.

If a crisp garnish is required – for example, a base for presenting prawn fritters or other dishes – use rice vermicelli straight from the packet, frying small amounts at a time in deep hot oil. The oil should be hot enough to make the rice vermicelli puff and whiten as soon as it is

if too hot, it will brown; so it does take a little practice to be able to judge the right heat. Lift out quickly on a wire strainer and drain on absorbent kitchen paper.

Fresh Rice Noodles with Sauce

Cut the rice noodles into thin strips. Put them into a bowl and cover with boiling water; cover the bowl and leave for 5 minutes. Drain in a colander.

Place the noodles in a large serving bowl, add all other ingredients and toss lightly until well mixed. Serve on a bed of shredded lettuce and garnish with tomato flowers and coriander.

This snack can be turned into a light meal by adding shreds of cooked pork, chicken, shelled prawns and bean sprouts, or chopped spring onions.

Serves 4
450 g (1 lb) twin rice
   noodles (chee cheong
   fun)
20 ml (4 tsp) Chinese
   barbecue sauce
20 ml (4 tsp) light soy
   sauce
20 ml (4 tsp) dark soy
   sauce
20 ml (4 tsp) oyster sauce
10 ml (2 tsp) sesame oil
10 ml (2 tsp) sweet chilli
   sauce
30 ml (2 tbsp) toasted
   sesame seeds

Cut rice noodles into slices.   *Drain the soaked noodles.*

Agar-Agar and Noodle Salad

It is possible to make a meatless version of this salad, substituting strips of bean curd for the chicken, or simply omitting it. An ideal cold dish for picnics or light meals.

Soak the agar-agar for at least 2 hours in cold water. Drain well and cut into finger-length strips. Cook the noodles in plenty of lightly salted boiling water until just tender, testing a piece every now and then to make sure they don't overcook. Run cold water into the pan and drain in a colander.

Combine the beaten eggs with salt and spring onions. Heat a small heavy frying pan. Pour 15 ml (1 tbsp) of peanut oil into a saucer, dip a piece of absorbent kitchen paper in it and lightly grease the base of the frying pan. Pour in just enough of the egg mixture to make a thin omelette; cook on low heat just until set, without browning, then turn it out on to a plate. Continue until all the egg is used. Allow to cool.

Heat a wok, add the remaining 15 ml (1 tbsp) of peanut oil and fry the garlic for a few seconds, not long enough to brown it. Add the bean sprouts and toss for 30 seconds, then remove from heat. Allow to cool.

In a large serving bowl, toss together the agar-agar, noodles, bean sprouts and chicken.

Combine the sesame oil and soy sauce to make a dressing, pour it over the ingredients in the bowl, and toss to distribute the dressing.

Roll up the omelettes (like a Swiss roll), cut them into narrow slices, and add to the bowl. Cover and refrigerate. Just before serving, garnish with the coriander and spring onions and strips of ham.

Serves 6
15 g (½ oz) refined agar-agar strips
225 g (8 oz) egg noodles
2 eggs, beaten
2.5 ml (½ tsp) salt
2 spring onions
30 ml (2 tbsp) peanut oil
2.5 ml (½ tsp) crushed garlic
225 g (8 oz) fresh bean sprouts
strips of cold, cooked chicken
45 ml (2 tbsp) sesame oil
60 ml (4 tbsp) light soy sauce
60 ml (4 tbsp) chopped fresh coriander leaves
60 ml (4 tbsp) sliced spring onions
matchstick strips of ham (optional)

Drain the agar-agar and cut into pieces.

Toss agar-agar, noodles, bean sprouts and chicken.

Roll up omelettes and cut into slices.

Sweets and Breads

Chinese meals don't feature desserts, but there is no denying it is a pleasant custom and most Chinese restaurants humour their patrons by providing something to end the meal on a sweet note such as Toffee Apples, Almond Bean Curd or that incredibly un-Chinese concoction, Fried Ice Cream.

Most often though, sweets are eaten as between-meal snacks. Chinese sweetmeats are turned out in factories and are quite cheap and easy to purchase. Don't expect the labels to enlighten you about the contents. 'Peanut Cake' for instance, is flat, crisp and rather similar to Middle Eastern halva. I have eaten it, freshly made, in eastern cities but it loses nothing when packaged in transparent paper and sealed in packets.

Then there are brittle, toffee-like bars of sesame seeds and sugar; deep fried cookies made of thin, crisp batter; flaky pastry or soft, freshly steamed yeast buns with fillings of sweet bean paste or lotus nut paste. Moon cakes, which sell by the thousand during the period leading up to the Moon Festival, are made from pastry pressed into a patterned wooden mould, filled with a solid core of chopped preserved fruits and nuts then richly glazed and baked. Those most prized have, in the centre, the yolk of a salted duck egg. Not to everyone's taste, perhaps.

There is also a variety of dried fruit, prettily wrapped in paper and labelled either 'Preserved Plum', 'Preserved Prune', or 'Honeyed Apricot'. They are sweet but also salty, a combination that is strange at first, then addictive. Dried lychees in their shells are totally different from the fresh or canned fruit. The shell becomes thin, brittle and easily cracked while the fruit has turned dark, rather like a large, round raisin.

Walnut and date 'cake' is a sticky, fudge-like creation but pleasant and not too sweet. A word of advice: some of these sweets are wrapped twice and the inner wrapping which looks like fine food wrap is really rice paper which is meant to be eaten with the sweet. Don't try to remove it – it defies all efforts.

Perhaps the most popular ending to a meal is fortune cookies. These too are sold in packets, but are so much nicer if freshly made so a simple recipe is included in this chapter. Here, too, are recipes for the buns, steamed breads and mandarin pancakes which are meant to be served with savoury dishes.

Left: *clockwise from front left: Fortune Cookies (see page 140), dried lychees, small peanut candies, dates, Steamed Flower Rolls (see page 143), almond flavoured cakes, dried plums (paper wrapped), moon cakes, deep fried pastries, dried plums, date toffee, sesame brittle, peanut cakes.*

Fortune Cookies

Makes 12–14
2 egg whites
75 g (3 oz) caster sugar
25 g (1 oz) cornflour
25 g (1 oz) flour
2.5 ml (½ tsp) vanilla
flavouring
5 ml (1 tsp) peanut oil

Have the 'fortunes' typed on short strips of paper, ready to enclose.

Preheat the oven to 180°C (350°F) mark 4. Prepare baking trays by brushing with oil and dusting with cornflour; tap off excess cornflour. Mark two circles about 9 cm (3½ inches) across, using a bowl or mug.

Lightly beat the egg whites just until frothy. Add the sugar and mix it in. Stir in sifted cornflour and flour. Add the vanilla flavouring and the peanut oil, and stir to combine. Place 10 ml (2 tsp) of the mixture on each circle and spread evenly with a knife.

Bake in the preheated oven for about 8 minutes or until evenly golden in colour. Immediately remove the cookies, one at a time. Place a 'fortune' on the cookie, press the edges together and bend the folded side of the cookie over the edge of a bowl to give it a twist. Immediately fold other biscuit. If it has firmed, return it to the oven to soften. If the biscuits are too hot for you to handle, use a cloth or oven mits. Allow to cool on wire racks, and store in an airtight container.

Spread cookie mixture on prepared trays.

Place 'fortune' in cookie and press edge together.

Bend cookie over edge of bowl.

Mandarin Pancakes

Serves 4–5
225 g (8 oz) flour
175 ml (6 fl oz) boiling
  water
20 ml (4 tsp) sesame oil

These delicate pancakes are traditionally served with Peking Duck, but are also used to enclose a variety of fillings such as shredded pork or chicken. The filling is seasoned with a dab of rich-flavoured sauce, then rolled up and eaten.

Measure the unsifted flour into a bowl. Bring water to the boil and pour at once on to the flour, stirring with chopsticks or the handle of a wooden spoon for a few minutes. As soon as it is cool enough to handle, knead for 10 minutes until the mixture is a soft, smooth dough. Put the dough on a board and cover with a bowl, then let it stand for at least 30 minutes.

Roll the dough into a cylindrical shape and cut it into ten slices of equal size. Keep covered with plastic wrap to prevent drying out.

Take one dough slice at a time and cut into two equal pieces. Form each to a smooth ball, then roll out on a lightly floured board to a circle about 8 cm (3 inches) in diameter. Brush one circle lightly with sesame oil, taking it right to the edge of the circle. Put the second circle on top of the first one and roll again, both circles together this time, until the pancakes are 15–18 cm (6–7 inches) across. They must be very thin. Cover each pancake with plastic as it is made.

When they are all rolled out, heat a heavy frying pan or griddle and cook the pancakes one at a time on the ungreased surface. Cook over low heat until the pancake develops small bubbles. Turn it frequently so that it cooks on both sides. A few golden spots will appear.

Remove from pan and gently pull the two circles apart. The sesame oil they were brushed with makes this quite easy. Pile the cooked pancakes on a plate, and cover tightly or they will dry out. Pancakes should be soft and pliable, not brittle.

To reheat, arrange the pancakes in a steamer lined with a clean tea towel, cover and put over simmering water for 1–2 minutes. To serve, fold each pancake into quarters.

Serve with Crisp Fried Boneless Duck (see page 101), Mu Shu Pork (page 113) and similar dishes.

Stir boiling water into flour using chopsticks.

Knead dough until soft and smooth.

Oil one circle of dough and cover with another.

The cooked pancakes separate easily.

Steamed Silver Thread Rolls

Makes 8 rolls
15 g (½ oz) fresh yeast
125 g (4½ oz) sugar
275 g (10 oz) flour
2.5 ml (½ tsp) baking
   powder
sesame oil

Brush rectangle of dough with sesame oil and fold in half lengthways.

Brush with more oil, fold again and cut into strips.

Place on an oblong-shaped piece of dough.

Bring edges together and pinch to join.

Crumble the yeast into a bowl, gradually stir in the sugar and then add 250 ml (8 fl oz) lukewarm water, stirring until sugar and yeast are dissolved.

Sift the flour and baking powder and add to liquid, mixing to a fairly firm dough. Knead on a floured surface for 5 minutes or until dough becomes smooth and elastic.

Rub a large bowl with a little oil and place the dough in the bowl, turning once so that the top of dough is lightly oiled. Cover with plastic wrap and leave in a warm place to rise until double in bulk (about 2 hours).

Turn the dough out on to a floured surface and knead for 5 minutes. Then divide it into 16 equal portions.

Roll one portion to an oblong shape 15 cm × 10 cm (6 inches × 4 inches). Brush lightly with sesame oil and fold in half lengthways, then brush with more oil and fold again. Cut into fine strips. Roll another portion of dough to a thick oblong shape, wide enough to wrap around the strips and about the same length. Place the strips on the oblong dough, bring its edges together and pinch to join them. Place seam side downwards.

Prepare seven more dough rolls in the same way. Leave to rise in a warm place for 30 minutes. Steam in a bamboo steamer for 15 minutes.

Serve with rich dishes such as Crisp Fried Boneless Duck (see page 101) and Mu Shu Pork (page 113).

Steamed Flower Rolls

Prepare the dough as for Silver Thread Rolls, leave it to rise for about 2 hours, knead a second time, then divide into halves. Set one portion aside.

On a lightly floured board, use a floured rolling pin to roll out one portion of dough to a rectangle 40 cm × 30 cm (16 inches × 12 inches). Brush the entire surface with sesame oil, then starting at the long side, roll up the dough to form a cylinder. Cut into 2.5 cm (1 inch) slices. There should be 16 of these.

Place one roll on top of another and with a chopstick press firmly in the centre. The rolled edges will open like the petals of a flower. Repeat, to make seven more dough flowers. Place in a lightly oiled steaming basket, and steam over boiling water for 8 to 10 minutes. Repeat with remaining portion of dough.

Rolls may be made beforehand and reheated by gently steaming for 2 to 3 minutes.

Note: If a bamboo steamer is not available, use a large saucepan and place the rolls on a plate above the water level, but line the lid with a tea towel to prevent condensation dropping on to the rolls and spoiling their appearance. Also, when steaming is finished, turn off the heat but leave for a minute or two before lifting the lid to prevent a rush of cold air causing the steamed dough to shrink or wrinkle.

Makes 16 rolls
15 g (½ oz) fresh yeast
125 g (4½ oz) sugar
275 g (10 oz) flour
2.5 ml (½ tsp) baking powder
sesame oil

Brush rectangle of dough with sesame oil and roll up.

Cut into slices.

Place one roll on top of another and press a chopstick firmly in the centre.

Steam in a lightly oiled basket for 8 to 10 minutes.

Wonton Wrappers

These are readily available in Chinese supermarkets, but if you can't get to one, or if you would like to try your hand at making them, here's how.

Sift the flour and salt into a large bowl. Make a well in the centre.

Beat the egg lightly with 125 ml (4 fl oz) water, and pour it into the well in the flour. Mixing from the centre, with a fork, gradually work in the flour. Knead into a ball, then turn it out on to a well-floured surface and knead the dough for 5 to 6 minutes until smooth. Cover with a damp cloth and leave to rest for 30 minutes.

Cut the dough into four portions, and roll each portion out on a well-floured surface. Using a ruler, cut dough into 8 cm (3 inch) squares. Stack in piles, dusting liberally with cornflour to prevent sticking. Wrap the piles in plastic and store in the refrigerator.

Cut dough into quarters and roll out.

Cut the thinly rolled-out dough into squares.

Makes 40–50 wrappers
225 g (8 oz) flour
2.5 ml (½ tsp) salt
1 egg
extra flour
cornflour

Deep Fried Date Wonton

These crisp sweetmeats will keep for a week in an airtight container.

Chop the dates finely. Chop the nuts too. Combine dates, nuts, grated rind and just enough juice to make the mixture hold together. Form into small cylinders which will fit on the pastry squares diagonally, leaving enough pastry to twist at each end like a cracker.

Place the date rolls on the pastry, take one corner and tuck it under, then roll up to enclose the filling. Twist the ends, putting a finger in the pastry to give it a Christmas cracker shape.

When all the wonton are wrapped, heat about 850 ml (1½ pints) peanut oil in a wok and fry a few at a time, turning them, until they are golden brown all over. Lift out with a wire spoon and drain on absorbent kitchen paper placed on a wire rack. When cool, sprinkle lightly with icing sugar. Store in an airtight container.

Note: If preferred, use canned lotus nut paste or sweet bean paste for the filling.

Makes about 50
225 g (8 oz) stoned dates
50 g (2 oz) walnuts or
    almonds
5 ml (1 tsp) finely grated
    orange rind
15 ml (1 tbsp) orange juice
225 g (8 oz) wonton pastry
    squares
peanut oil for deep frying
icing sugar for dusting

Twist ends of filled pastries.

Sesame Balls

Makes 20
100 g (4 oz) stoned dates
45 ml (3 tbsp) sesame
   paste
350 g (12 oz) sweet
   potatoes
150 g (5 oz) flour
75 ml (5 tbsp) brown sugar
1 egg white
150 g (5 oz) sesame seeds
peanut oil for deep frying

Put the dates into a small saucepan with water to cover. Bring to the boil and boil for 1 minute. Drain, then mash the dates to a paste. Blend in the sesame paste.

Peel the sweet potatoes, cut them into chunks. Put them into a saucepan with water to cover, bring to the boil and simmer for 20 to 30 minutes until the potato is tender. Drain well, then mash and force through a sieve. Weigh out 275 g (10 oz).

Sift 100 g (4 oz) of the flour into a bowl, add the sweet potato and mix with a fork. The mixture will be lumpy at this stage.

Heat the sugar with 15 ml (1 tbsp) of water until boiling, stirring to dissolve the sugar. Add this hot syrup to the flour and potato mixture. Form it into a dough, adding a little more flour if necessary. Knead lightly on a floured surface for 1 minute.

Divide the dough evenly into 20 portions and roll each portion into a ball. Flatten the ball with the palm of your hand. Place a teaspoon of the date-sesame mixture in the centre. Shape into a ball, completely enclosing the paste. Repeat with the remaining dough and filling.

Place the balls in an oiled steaming basket and steam over gently boiling water for 10 minutes.

Dip the balls in lightly beaten egg white and then roll them in sesame seeds.

Heat a wok, add oil for deep frying. When hot, fry the sesame balls until golden. Drain and serve warm or cold.

Put spoonful of date filling on flattened dough.

Steam the balls in an oiled basket.

Dip the balls in egg white and roll in sesame seeds.

Toffee Yams with Black Sesame Seeds

This is a popular dessert and impressive. It may also be done with apple or with firm ripe bananas, peeled and cut into chunks but not pre-cooked.

Peel the sweet potatoes and cut them into diagonal slices. Drop them into a large saucepan of boiling water for 5 minutes. Drain and cool.

Beat the egg in a medium-sized bowl, add 150 ml (¼ pint) of cold water, and beat again until combined. Then tip in all the flour at once and beat vigorously until the batter is smooth. Allow the batter to stand while preparing the glaze.

Glaze: Heat the oil in a saucepan, add the sugar and 125 ml (4 fl oz) cold water. Place the saucepan over medium heat. Do not stir at all. If you do, the sugar will crystallize and the glaze will not be clear. Let the sugar mixture bubble until it starts to turn golden around the edge of the pan. Then stir in the sesame seeds and turn the heat as low as it will go. Or remove the saucepan from heat, replacing it from time to time if sugar begins to harden before the sweet potatoes have been dipped.

As the sugar cooks, start to heat the oil for deep frying. Try to have the oil hot and the sugar glaze ready (that is, deep golden) at the same time. If the oil is put over a moderate heat, this should not be difficult.

When a haze begins to rise from the surface of the oil, drop pieces of sweet potato into the batter, turn to coat them completely, then take one piece at a time with chopsticks, a fondue fork or fingers and drop it into the oil. Deep fry until the batter is golden, then lift out with a slotted spoon and put it straight into the saucepan containing the glaze. Do two or three pieces at a time, turn them so that the glaze coats their entire surface, then lift out on to an oiled plate.

Take immediately to the table, together with a bowl containing cold water and ice cubes. Each person takes a piece of glazed yam and drops it into the bowl. The glaze will harden and become brittle almost at once. Lift out quickly and eat. If left to stand too long, the glaze will melt and the batter will become leathery.

Serves 6
450 g (1 lb) sweet potatoes
1 egg
100 g (4 oz) flour
peanut oil for deep frying
Glaze:
5 ml (1 tsp) peanut oil
350 g (12 oz) sugar
20 ml (4 tsp) black sesame
    seeds

Deep fry the battered yams until golden.

Glaze 2 to 3 pieces of yam at a time and lift onto an oiled plate.

Guests dip glazed yams into cold water before eating.

Almond Bean Curd

Serves 4–6
**20 ml (4 tsp) powdered
  agar-agar**
**400 g (14 oz) can
  sweetened condensed
  milk**
**5–10 ml (1–2 tsp) almond
  essence**

Put 1 litre (1¾ pints) water into a saucepan, sprinkle the agar-agar over and bring to the boil. Boil and stir until the agar-agar is dissolved. Powdered agar takes only a couple of minutes to dissolve.

Add the condensed milk and almond essence, and stir well. Pour the mixture into a large shallow glass dish or a large cake tin. Allow it to cool and set, then chill.

Cut it into cubes or diamond shapes, and serve by itself or with canned fruits or freshly made melon balls.

The agar-agar powder and dried strands of agar-agar.

Cut the chilled mixture into shapes.

Glossary

ABALONE: This marine mollusc is a prized seafood among Chinese and Japanese. Its single shell has a beautiful iridescent interior and the edible portion is the large round foot with which it attaches itself to rocks. When purchased raw it has to be cut in thin slices, tenderised by beating with a meat mallet, and sautéed for less than a minute to prevent toughening. It is more easily available in cans, already tenderised and cooked. Simply slice and marinate or, for hot dishes, add at the last minute to prevent it becoming tough. Japanese and Mexican abalone are usually best.

AGAR-AGAR: A setting agent made from seaweed. Available in powder form in packets from Asian grocery stores. Also available in strands. Use either type for jellies, but for dishes like Agar-Agar and Noodle Salad, only the strands are suitable. See photograph on page 147.

BAMBOO SHOOT: Sold in cans either water-packed or braised. Unless otherwise stated, the recipes in this book call for the water-packed variety. After opening can, store in a bowl of fresh water in the refrigerator, replacing water daily, for up to 10 days. Winter bamboo shoots are much smaller and more tender, but if they are not available, the larger variety can be used.

BEAN CURD: (dow foo) Fresh soft bean curd, made from soy beans, is available in the refrigerator section of Asian stores, ready to use. Immersed in cold water which should be changed daily, it will keep for 2 to 3 days in the refrigerator. It has a soft, custard-like texture. See photograph on page 74. No substitute.

Dried bean curd: (tiem jook, fu jook pei) Comes in thin, flat sheets or rounded sticks. Needs no refrigeration, keeps indefinitely in wrapping or jar, needs to be soaked before use.

Fried bean curd: (dow foo pok) Sold in the refrigerator section in Asian stores, usually in plastic bags. See photograph on page 50. Can be kept under refrigeration for 3 or 4 days.

Hard bean curd: (pressed bean curd) Also sold fresh, is firmer and has a different flavour. See photograph on page 50. Good protein in vegetarian meals. Store in refrigerator for 2 or 3 days. Canned variety may be used in braised dishes, but the fresh is infinitely better.

Red bean curd: (nam yu) Also known as bean curd cheese because it is fermented and very strong flavoured. Used in small amounts to add flavour to special dishes. See photograph on page 100. Keeps indefinitely in jar.

BEAN SAUCES: There are many kinds of bean sauce, salty, sweet and hot. The most basic are mor sze jeung (ground bean sauce), smooth and thick, and min sze jeung, a thick paste of mashed and whole fermented soy beans. The most popular sweet bean sauce is hoi sin jeung. The hot bean sauces (mostly used in Szechwan style dishes) are chilli bean sauce, hot bean sauce and soy chilli sauce. Some are oily, some are not. All these bean sauces are too thick to pour. Use the one specified in the recipe for the best results.

BEAN PASTE (SAUCE), SWEET: Sweet and salty thick sauce or paste which is sold in jars and keeps indefinitely. See photograph on page 19. Depending on which brand you buy, it could be described as 'paste' or 'sauce' or 'sweet ground bean sauce'. Play it safe and also look for the Chinese name which is tin min jeung to distinguish this sauce from dow saah the sweet bean paste (also called 'sweetened black bean paste' or 'sweet mashed bean paste') which is used as a filling for steamed buns.

BEAN SPROUTS: Green mung beans are used for bean sprouts. They are sold fresh in most Chinese stores and in certain supermarkets and health food stores. The canned variety are not recommended. Substitute thinly sliced celery for crunchy texture, though flavour is differ-ent. Fresh bean sprouts may be stored in refrigerator for a week in plastic bag, or cover with water and change water daily.

BEAN STARCH NOODLES: Also known as bean threads or cellophane noodles. Fine transparent noodles made from the starch of green mung beans. See photograph on page 35. They may be soaked in hot water or boiled, or for a crisp garnish are deep fried straight from the packet. Cut with scissors—they're tough.

BEAN STARCH SHEETS: Made from green mung beans, these round sheets are soaked in hot water, then cooked until soft. See photographs on page 28. Sold in Chinese stores in plastic bags, in dried form the starch sheets keep indefinitely.

BLACK BEANS, SALTED: Soy beans, heavily salted and preserved in cans. See photograph on page 79. Rinse before using to prevent oversalting. After opening, store in refrigerator, for as long as six months. Pour a little peanut oil on top if it seems to dry out.

CHILLI OIL: Sold in small bottles, it is oil impregnated with the pungent flavour of chillies and is used in small amounts. Keeps for about a month after opening. If unobtainable, make some by heating about a cup of oil in a wok and adding some dried red chillies. If using the large chillies, use 12 and if using the small chillies, which are much hotter, use less. Fry the chillies for a minute or so, until they turn dark, remove wok from heat and leave until quite cold before straining the oil and storing in a bottle.

CHILLI SAUCE: Chinese chilli sauce is different from other chilli sauce. Substitute Tabasco or other hot pepper sauce, not one of the sweet chilli sauces. Keeps indefinitely.

CHILLI SAUCE, SWEET: Milder but still fairly pungent, the sweetened chilli sauce usually has added garlic and ginger. Substitute either unsweetened chilli sauce mixed with a little sugar, crushed garlic and ginger, or tomato sauce with a generous dash of Tabasco.

CHINESE CABBAGE: There are a number of Chinese vegetables which are all called 'cabbage' but are quite different in appearance and flavour. Each has been photographed in the recipe to make identification easy, but here are descriptions which may help when purchasing.

Bok choy: Chinese chard, with silvery white leaf ribs and very dark green leaves, it is one of the milder flavoured vegetables. See photograph on page 52.

Gai choy: Mustard cabbage, so called because of its strong, mustardy tang. Recognise it by its brilliant green colour and the way its leaves curve from the central stalk. See photograph on page 30.

Gai larn: Chinese broccoli or kale. Dark green stems and leaves, with white flowers. Select young plants with buds rather than flowers. Thicker stems may need peeling and splitting. See photograph on page 36.

Wongah bak: The most popular, widely known Chinese cabbage is variously called Tientsin cabbage, celery cabbage and Peking cabbage. It is most delicate in flavour and has broad white leaf ribs with pale green leaves packed together tightly. It may be eaten raw, but most often is lightly cooked with other ingredients. See photograph on page 37.

Choy sum: Flowering cabbage, rather like gai larn in appearance but its flowers are yellow and the stems do not have a thick tough skin. See photograph on page 104.

Like all members of the cabbage family, Chinese cabbages are most plentiful in the cooler months. Soak in cold water and wash very well, especially where the leaves join the stem, to ensure all sand and any insecticides are rinsed away. All Chinese vegetables should be cooked briefly so their colour intensifies and the texture remains crisp.

CHINESE VINEGAR: (ba tso) There is more than one kind of Chinese vinegar, some light in colour, others quite dark, sweet and spicy. Used in cooking or as a dip. Substitute: these vinegars are milder than western wine or cider vinegars, so quantities must be adjusted or vinegar diluted if a substitution is made.

CHINESE WINE: (Shao hsing) Rice wine which may be substituted with dry sherry.

CORIANDER, FRESH: (Chinese parsley) This is the green herb as distinct from the dried seeds used as a spice in curry mixtures. Dark green, with leaves resembling flat Italian parsley, this pungent herb is used widely in Chinese cooking. See photograph on page 132. Store in tightly closed plastic bags in crisper section of refrigerator. Really fresh bunches which have not been wet (or if they have, are thoroughly dried on absorbent paper) will keep for about two weeks. No substitute for flavour, but use parsley for a garnish.

CUCUMBER SLICES IN SYRUP, PRESERVED: Rather like shoelace shreds of melon and carrot in a heavy syrup, they are also sometimes labelled 'sweet pickled cucumber' or 'preserved melon shreds'. See photograph on page 68. They will keep indefinitely in a covered jar. No substitute.

DRIED SHRIMP: Used as a seasoning rather than a main ingredient, because drying gives them a concentrated flavour. Soak as directed. Sold by weight in packets, they keep almost indefinitely in sealed packets or in a tightly covered jar after opening. No substitute.

FISH MAW, DRIED: (fish tripe, yu toe) The dried stomach lining of large fish, it is purely a texture ingredient, has no fishy taste or smell and looks, in its dried state, like a puffy, cream-coloured sponge. See photograph on page 45. Soak as directed in individual recipes. No substitute.

FIVE SPICE POWDER: A combination of ground anise, fennel, cinnamon, cloves and Szechwan pepper, it gives distinctive flavour in cooking and is also used as a dip, combined with salt. Inexpensive, keeps well in tightly covered jar.

GARLIC CHIVES: (koo chye or gau choi) these long, flat green leaves have a strong flavour, half-way between garlic and spring onions. Store in paper in the crisper section of the refrigerator. Some Chinese stores sell these together with other fresh vegetables.

GINGER ROOT: A basic seasoning in Chinese food. Buy fresh root ginger from Chinese food shops, greengrocers, supermarkets. Store by freezing in a plastic bag, peeling and bottling in a jar of dry sherry (store in refrigerator); or burying in moist soil and watering frequently. Dig up a piece as needed, replace remaining ginger root in soil and keep moist. If you are able to buy it frequently, store in the crisper section of the refrigerator where it will keep fresh for about three weeks. Ginger is also available sliced in cans and this is the best substitute for fresh ginger. Do not use powdered ginger as a substitute.

GINGER, RED: Ginger slices in heavy syrup, coloured a bright red. Add to Chinese dishes as a flavouring and garnish. No substitute.

GLUTEN: Gluten is the protein part of wheat, and a very fine flour made from it is available in health food stores. Prepare as described on page 53. Used in vegetarian dishes, it is a meat substitute and absorbs other flavours though it has very little flavour of its own. Fried bean curd is a reasonable substitute.

HOI SIN SAUCE: A thick, sweet, spicy, reddish brown sauce made from beans, garlic, spices. Keeps well in a covered jar.

HOKKIEN MEE: Mee is the word for noodles and Hokkien Mee are thick yellow wheat noodles sold fresh, not dried. They are ready-cooked and need only to be immersed for a few seconds in boiling water, or have boiling water poured over them in a colander, just to heat through.

KUMQUATS IN SYRUP: Most commonly sold in 390g jars, these tangy citrus fruits go well with salty sauces. See photograph on page 115. If you have a kumquat tree, you could try using the fresh fruit, first removing the seeds. Keeps well in its own jar and needs no refrigeration. Substitute glacé orange slices.

LAP CHEONG: Dried Chinese-style sausages filled only with spiced and slightly sweetened lean and fat pork. See photograph on page 129. Will keep without refrigeration. Steam for 10 minutes until soft and plump, cut into thin slices to serve or to include in dishes. Quite expensive compared to ordinary western style sausages because they contain no fillers. Substitute barbecued pork.

LILY BUDS, DRIED: (Also known as golden needles, dried tiger lillies) these dried buds are long and narrow with a delicate flavour. They are said to be nutritious. See photograph on page 113. Sold in cellophane packets, they need at least 30 minutes soaking in hot water. Will keep well if stored in an airtight jar. Substitute another bland vegetable, or omit from recipe.

LONG BEANS: Pictured on page 63, these are sometimes known as snake beans or yard beans. Dark green, thin beans are preferable to thicker, paler green ones as they are sweeter and more tender. Substitute very tender young French beans.

LOTUS ROOT: Sometimes available fresh. Peel, cut into slices and use as directed. See photograph on page 114. Dried lotus root keeps well, must be soaked in hot water for at least 20 minutes, with lemon juice added to preserve whiteness. Canned lotus root is readily available, but for the recipes in this book you don't buy the canned lotus root in sugar syrup.

MELON, BITTER: (Fu gwa) This gourd looks like a green cucumber but with a pebbly-textured, very glossy skin. See photograph on page 108. When ripe it is a pretty golden colour with bright red seeds, but the time to eat it is when it is green in colour and only half mature. The flavour is bitter, but pleasantly so, combining well with strong-flavoured sauces and meat or seafood. No substitute.

MELON, FUZZY: Pale green, rounded ends with a narrower centre, the fuzzy melon is about a handspan in length and, true to its name, has a covering of prickly white fuzz. See photograph on page 44. Scrub well and peel thinly so the flesh is still tinged with green. It may be used interchangeably with winter melon as the texture and delicate flavour is very similar. Substitute peeled, seeded cucumbers.

MELON, WINTER: A dark green, watermelon-like gourd which can grow up to 50kg in weight! No wonder it is usually sold by the slice. The neutral flesh takes flavours from other ingredients. Substitute fuzzy melon or cucumber.

MUSHROOMS, DRIED CHINESE: There are two types of dried Chinese mushrooms, one which is called Flower Mushroom because of the petal-like indentations on its upper surface. The caps of these mushrooms are thicker and meatier than the other type which are sometimes known as 'love letters' or winter mushrooms. The flavour is similar, but flower mushrooms are more expensive. However, they are the best kind to use because of their chewy texture. Dried mushrooms keep indefinitely in a closed packet or jar, are sold by weight (sometimes in packets or boxes) and though the price seems frighteningly high, a

little goes a long way and even the tough stems and soaking water (they need at least 30 minutes soaking in very hot water) can be used to flavour stocks. See photograph on page 23. No substitute. Do not substitute dried European mushrooms, the flavour is different.

OYSTER SAUCE: Adds delicate flavour to all kinds of dishes. Made from oysters cooked in soy sauce and brine, this thick brown sauce keeps indefinitely. Once opened, store in refrigerator.

PEPPERY TURNIPS, (chilli radish): A strong-flavoured condiment which is used in some dishes to give a fiery tang. See photograph on page 89. Keeps well in covered jar. Substitute small amount of chilli bean sauce.

PICKLES, CHINESE MIXED: Small onions, gherkins, cucumber, ginger and other selected vegetables in a vinegar, sugar and salt pickling mixture. See photograph on page 96. Substitute pickled gherkins and onions if necessary.

PLUM SAUCE: Sweet and spicy and sometimes slightly hot, this sauce is based on plums, chillies, vinegar, spices and sugar. Use as a dip. Keeps indefinitely in a covered jar.

ROCK SUGAR: Pale amber lumps of raw sugar which are used to give a subtle sweetness and glaze to some dishes. See photograph on page 13. Since it comes in quite large pieces, wrap one in a cloth and crush with a meat mallet before measuring. Substitute granulated sugar or raw sugar crystals.

SAMBAL ULEK: This paste of hot fresh red chillies is the easy way to adding the pungency of ground chillies without the work and the burning fingers. Sometimes labelled in the old Dutch Indonesian way, 'sambal oelek'. Same thing. Keeps well. After opening, store in refrigerator.

SESAME OIL: This oil is extracted from toasted sesame seeds, giving it a rich amber colour and totally different flavour from the lighter sesame oil sometimes sold in health stores. For the recipes in this book, purchase sesame oil from Chinese stores. Use in small quantities for flavouring, not as a cooking medium.

SHARK FIN: Unless you want to precede the eating with three days' work, use the canned shark fin! See photograph on page 40. The dried fins are very expensive, must be soaked and cooked for hours. Even the canned fins (which are split into shreds of gelatinous cartilage) are not exactly cheap. Substitute boiled bean starch noodles if you must, but shark fin is a prestige ingredient for banqueting and no substitute is really acceptable.

SNOW PEAS: Also known as sugar peas. Sold fresh in season, these are mainly a speciality of Chinese market gardeners but large seed companies now sell the seeds in packets under the name of sugar peas. They are never cooked for longer than a minute or two and are eaten pod and all. The French name for them is mange-tout. They are sometimes available frozen, but lack the delightful crispness of the fresh peas. Store fresh snow peas for a few days in a plastic bag or in a bowl of water in the refrigerator.

SOY SAUCE: Indispensable in Chinese cooking, this versatile sauce enhances the flavour of every basic ingredient in a dish. Different grades are available. Dark soy sauce is used in most instances, but light soy is used when cooking chicken or seafood, or in soups where the delicate flavour and colour of the dish must be preserved. Keeps indefinitely. Usually sold in large or small bottles, but if purchased in a can, decant into a bottle.

SPRING ROLL WRAPPERS: Thin, white sheets of pastry sold in plastic packets. Usually frozen. Unused wrappers may be refrozen. Large wonton wrappers may not be substituted.

STAR ANISE: One of the prettiest seed pods, it looks like a reddish brown, eight-petalled flower. See photograph on page 121. Used in stocks or master sauces for red-cooked dishes, it imparts a licorice flavour. Keeps indefinitely in covered jar. Inexpensive. No substitute.

STRAW MUSHROOMS: Unlike dried mushrooms with their strong flavour, these mushrooms are as delicately flavoured as champignons. They are shrouded in their own little 'tent' which envelops the stalk and cap with a thin skin. Sold in cans. See photograph on page 94.

SZECHWAN PEPPERCORNS: Also known as anise pepper, Chinese pepper, faah jiu. A small reddish-brown dried berry, smaller than black peppercorns and not as hot. They give a tingling, numbing sensation when placed on the tongue. See photograph on page 92. Dry roast in a dry pan until fragrant, about 5 minutes over low heat, stirring now and then. Pound in mortar and pestle or with cleaver. Keeps well in an airtight bottle.

TANGERINE PEEL, DRIED: (gom pei) Gives citrus fragrance to dishes. Expensive, so when mandarins or tangerines are in season, save the peel, scrape away any white pith and dry the peel in the sun or in a very low oven. Store airtight. Fresh peel may be used as a substitute.

TWIN RICE NOODLES: Chee cheong fun. These already cooked rice noodles look for all the world like two rolled-up white linen handkerchiefs wrapped in plastic. See photograph on page 123. They need only to be sliced through and heated either by pouring boiling water over or by steaming in a colander before combining with other ingredients. Look for them in the refrigerator section of Asian food stores. If not in stock, substitute sa ho fun (rice noodles in flat sheets, folded) which are also treated the same way before incorporating in a recipe. They are sometimes used as a wrapping for a savoury filling. Keep refrigerated for a few days.

WALNUTS: Peeled walnuts are sold by weight in Chinese grocery stores and are perfect for using in fried dishes, as the thin skin which turns bitter through cooking has been removed. If peeled walnuts are not available, use the canned, salted walnuts also sold in Chinese stores. These do not need further cooking.

WATER CHESTNUTS: Sometimes available fresh, the brownish-black skin must be peeled away with a sharp knife, leaving the crisp, slightly sweet kernel. Available in cans, already peeled. After opening, store in water in refrigerator for a week changing water daily. No substitute. See photograph on page 118.

WONTON WRAPPERS: Small squares of fresh noodle dough bought from Chinese stores. Refrigerate, well wrapped in plastic, for a week. See photograph on page 230.

WOOD FUNGUS: (Cloud ears, tree ears, wun yee, jelly mushrooms.) Sold by weight, wood fungus in its dry state looks like greyish black pieces of paper. Soaked in water for 10 minutes, it swells to translucent brown shapes which explains why it is called 'cloud ear'. See photograph on page 35. No flavour, but its resilience is greatly prized as a texture ingredient and it takes on flavours from other foods. Cook only a minute or two. Keeps indefinitely in dried form, and for a few days in the refrigerator after soaking. No substitute.

Index